W9-BJP-827

# GHOST STORIES
## *of*
# VIRGINIA

Dan Asfar

LONE
PINE

Lone Pine Publishing International

© 2006 by Lone Pine Publishing International Inc.
First printed in 2006 10 9 8 7 6 5 4 3 2 1
Printed in Canada

All rights reserved. No part of this work covered by the copyrights hereon may be reproduced or used in any form or by any means—graphic, electronic or mechanical—without the prior written permission of the publishers, except for reviewers, who may quote brief passages. Any request for photocopying, recording, taping or storage on information retrieval systems of any part of this work shall be directed in writing to the publisher.

**The Publisher: Lone Pine Publishing International**
Distributed by Lone Pine Publishing
1808 B Street NW, Suite 140
Auburn, WA 98001
USA

**Websites:** www.lonepinepublishing.com
www.ghostbooks.net

**National Library of Canada Cataloguing in Publication Data**

Asfar, Dan, 1973-
  Ghost stories of Virginia / Dan Asfar.

  ISBN-13: 978-976-8200-19-8
  ISBN-10: 976-8200-19-7

  1. Ghosts--Virginia.  2. Tales--Virginia.  I. Title.

GR110.V8A84 2006     398.209755'05     C2006-903202-5

*Photo Credits:* Every effort has been made to accurately credit photographers. Any errors or omissions should be directed to the publisher for changes in future editions. The photographs and illustrations in this book are reproduced with the kind permission of the following sources: Dan Brandenburg (p. 18);  Jim Jurica (p. 197); Andrew Kazmierski (p. 140); Library of Congress (p. 41: USZ62-116074); p. 56: D4-18387; p. 62: HABS VA,7-ALEX,44-2; p. 69: D4-33908; p. 74: DIG-cwpb-02510; p. 81: B8184-10376; p. 84: DIG-cwpb-01543; p. 95: USZ62-15135; p. 109: USZ62-15630; p. 202: B2-574-6); Pauline Wilson (p. 190).

The stories, folklore and legends in this book are based on the author's collection of sources including individuals whose experiences have led them to believe they have encountered phenomena of some kind or another. They are meant to entertain, and neither the publisher nor the author claims these stories represent fact.

*PC:* P5

*To Barbara Corbin,*
*for cooking the fish*

# Contents

# Acknowledgments

Firstly, I'd like to thank those who went out of their way to share their experiences with me. Although most of you preferred to remain anonymous, your accounts were greatly appreciated and added much to the stories in this volume. In addition, it would be remiss of me not to mention those authors who have gone before me on the subject of ghosts in Virginia. There is the inimitable guru of Virginia folklore, L.B. Taylor, Jr., whose expansive series of nonfiction ghost stories went beyond a thorough exploration of the supernatural in the Old Dominion and into its history and essence. *The Ghosts of Virginia,* volumes 1 and 2, as well as *The Ghosts of Williamsburg,* volume 2, were especially helpful, informing and inspiring more than one tale in this book. Also, thanks to the work of the late Marguerite Dupont Lee and her seminal volume *Virginia Ghosts,* which was a rich and fascinating historical document on the subject of folklore in Virginia.

Lastly, kudos as well to the people at Lone Pine International: Robert Sandiford, who helped work the kinks out of the text, Willa Kung, designer extraordinaire, and Carol Woo, our tireless and skilled researcher. Thanks.

# Introduction

Have you looked around lately? Ghosts are everywhere. Or maybe it would be more accurate to say that ghost *stories* are everywhere. Although the existence of ghosts is largely up for debate and generally frowned upon by the prevailing rationalism of our time, the ghost story is unarguably prevalent in the world of entertainment. On television and in film, psychic mediums abound. As a viewing audience, we are constantly being offered Hollywood actors gracefully and heroically transmitting messages from beyond the grave, whether it's Jennifer Love Hewitt, Patricia Arquette or Haley Joel Osment. In books, it is no different. Authors such as Stephen King, John Carpenter and Neil Gaiman have all taken on the supernatural in many of their works. One thing seems clear: we love ghost stories.

Not that that is anything new. As long as people have been putting pen to paper, there have been ghosts in popular storytelling. There are ghosts in Homer's *Iliad,* in the plays of William Shakespeare, in the short stories of Edgar Allan Poe, in the poetry of John Keats. And let us not forget the undying dead—the vampires of Bram Stoker and Anne Rice, Mary Shelley Wollstonecraft's Frankenstein, the armies of brain-eating corpses in countless zombie flicks.

One of the interesting things about the supernatural in entertainment is how the notion of ghosts says something about who we are as people. Although there's no arguing that the dead have always occupied a big place in cultural expression, the inevitability of death and the question of what follows forms one of the biggest questions, or perhaps *the* biggest question, regarding the human condition. Cultures near and far, remote and cosmopolitan, might be partly understood by the way their religious beliefs and folkloric narratives tackle the notion of the afterlife.

In the end, ghost stories are so popular because, whether we are prone to dwell on it or not, death concerns us all. And even if you believe that nothing but oblivion follows, it cannot be denied that any culture can be largely defined by the way it approaches the idea of death. What does this say about our contemporary culture, then, that a belief in ghosts is so widely accepted in entertainment, while generally rejected in reality? If, as most level-headed Americans would likely state, there is no such thing as ghosts, then why do we continue to be so fascinated by them?

The following pages do not attempt to tackle such questions. This is a book of ghost stories, nothing more, and it probably goes without saying that you didn't pick it up with hopes of coming to grips with such issues. Yet not one of the tales in this book was hatched from the whimsy of my imagination. All of these stories are said to be true—supernatural accounts told by Virginians, ghostly folklore that has survived the centuries, some of them well known, others more obscure—each and every one of them purported to have its roots in fact, rather than fancy. These are Virginia's ghost stories; I can only claim to be a faithful chronicler of some of the haunts in its history, the uncanny experiences of its citizens. It is up to you to decide whether or not to believe.

# 1
# Ghosts
# Through
# The Years

# The Ghosts of Bladensfield

At one time, it was said there were so many of them that a person could scarcely go from the front door to the parlor without bumping into one. Rattling chains, disembodied footsteps, cold spots, angry apparitions, stifling odors, burning orbs of light—residents and servants within Bladensfield's stately walls had to deal with such occurrences daily. It had been this way for as long as anyone could remember. Then, sometime in the late 1800s, the patriarch of the ancient home decided that something had to be done. Just because Bladensfield's history had it teeming with restless spirits since before the Civil War—before, some even said, the War of Independence—did not mean that nothing could be done about it. The patriarch was a devout Baptist, and he knew he had options. There were people he could talk to.

The Baptist preacher arrived at Bladensfield with a preternatural resolve—his head high, his jaw set. The patriarch, his family and servants were all outside around the front of the house when he arrived, but the preacher did not even look at them as he walked through the crowd. He made his way to the back of the house, the Bladensfield residents close behind. That was where he prepared himself for the ordeal—solemnly taking his coat off, turning it inside out and putting it back on upside down, so that the collar hung down his back and the tail was bunched up around his head.

There were a few snickers from among those assembled, but they were quickly silenced by a stern look from the patriarch. The preacher withdrew a worn, leather-bound Bible from a bag, took a deep breath and walked toward the door.

Behind him, the crowd followed, whispering in wonder or else still snickering at how serious the preacher was despite his inside-out, upside-down coat. Devout as the owner of Bladensfield may have been, he might have paused to think twice about the wisdom of turning to the clergy here after seeing the preacher's absurd get-up. If so, he swallowed these doubts and went along with the crowd, quelling some of the less pious with hard stares.

The priest began. Reaching into his inside—which was now outside—pocket, he produced a pair of reading glasses and perched them on his nose. He flipped through his Bible, quickly finding the right page. He stood there for a long moment, his eyes sweeping the room, took a deep breath, cast his gaze down on the book in his hands and began to read.

And yet he was making no sense. A low buzz came from the crowd behind him as servants and residents looked at one another in surprise, wondering what the jumble of words could mean. It didn't take long, however, for everyone to figure out what was happening. The words were familiar, but the order was wrong. The preacher was reading the Holy Scripture backward—starting from the bottom of the page and moving up, from the right side of the page to the left.

No one snickered anymore. The spectacle was suddenly unsettling—this man of God, a respected man in the community, standing there as serious as could be, with his coat rumpled ludicrously upon his back, reading the Bible backward. The more religiously inclined among the spectators made the sign of the cross and walked out, while the rest stood and stared with wide-eyed incredulity. In one room after another, the preacher made his rounds through the house, bestowing his blessing backward the whole time.

It is not known how the patriarch reacted to this bizarre display. Was he a traditional man? If so, it is entirely possible he did not approve. Perhaps in private he berated the preacher for such an exhibition. Or he may have just as easily been skeptical, indifferent, even amused. The same could be said for the rest of the people who witnessed the exorcism at Bladensfield. If any of them had regular encounters with unnatural forces in the house, there is no way to know if they would put any faith at all in a preacher whose solution to the problem was to rearrange his coat and read the Bible backward.

In any case, it is said that the strange events at Bladensfield lessened considerably after the preacher's visit. Everyone noticed it immediately. Used to hearing phantom footsteps in the hall almost every day, people could now walk without feeling as though they were being followed by some invisible presence. Likewise, the chill in the stairwell was felt less often and the house's famous apparitions appeared far less frequently. It seemed as though the ghosts of Bladensfield, which had run riot for so long, had been silenced.

Silenced, maybe, but not expelled. Indeed, it would take more than a preacher reading backward to exorcise the ghosts from Bladensfield.

One of the oldest standing structures in one of the oldest settled places in the United States, this Westmoreland County house has a history that is as sketchy and haunted as it is long. Although no one can state with any certainty the exact date the foundations were laid, one thing is sure—there have always been ghosts.

One of the more popular accounts places Bladensfield's provenance in the late 17th century. This account has the building commissioned by a colonial named Nicholas Rochester sometime in the 1690s. If true, this date would make Bladensfield among the oldest standing homes in Virginia's Northern Neck. Yet this information is contradicted by the Virginia Landmarks Register, which links Bladensfield to a man named Robert Carter who, the record tells us, constructed the house in the late 1700s.

Late 1700s or late 1600s? Some have offered that both dates might be correct. Carter may have constructed his home around the older structure commissioned by Rochester a century earlier. Yet whether Bladensfield is closer to two or three hundred years old, there is no argument as to its better-known residents.

No one disputes that the diligent and foul-tempered John Peck moved into Bladensfield in 1790, where he studied tirelessly and tutored the children of his wealthy neighbors. Peck owned Bladensfield for over 60 years, until the mid-19th century, when it was sold to Reverend William Norvell Ward. At this time, the house was expanded and made into a school for girls.

Definitely the most popular apparition was the one in the study. Seen most often by the house slaves, it was described as a stern-looking man seated before a desk, with a dull, amber glow emanating from his chest, smoldering underneath his stiff black coat. There was always a smell that accompanied sightings of this glowering apparition—a faint, sulfurous odor that filled the room.

It didn't take long for people to start spinning tales about how the apparition was none other than the spirit of John Peck. A tortured man driven by an obsessive need for work, he expected the same of his household and was a brutal taskmaster. He was known to be especially hard on his slaves, forcing them to constant and merciless labor that was excessive even by the ugly standards of the time. It made sense to Bladensfield slaves that such a man, unable to find peace while alive, would continue his restless and rancorous ways in death. As for the smell of sulfur, everyone knew where evil men went when they died and what that place was said to smell like.

The apparition, as described, certainly looked unhappy enough to be cursed with an eternity of fire and brimstone. Sometimes, when he was especially ornery, he would get up and move toward startled onlookers, the sound of rattling chains filling the room as he lumbered forward. It became so that whenever anyone heard chains rattling in Bladensfield, which was frequently enough, it was just assumed that John Peck was back again, festering away in the dark shadows. He was not the only one. The legend tells us that when John Peck wasn't creeping out people in his study, several other, less-agitated spirits called Bladensfield home. In an old bedroom upstairs, the ghost of Peck's daughter Alice was filling people fortunate enough to encounter her with a profound sense of peace and well-being.

According to one popular account, Alice inherited none of the hateful characteristics of her father. A beautiful young woman who lit up the estate with her natural grace and charm, she was the pride of Bladensfield, doted on by the household servants and the only one able to pierce her father's hard shell. Naturally, everyone was concerned when she took up with a local rakehell who, until he had caught Alice's eye, seemed destined for a life of easy leisure and drunken mischief.

His name has been forgotten, but he was said to be something of a leader among the gaming men in that region, a charismatic ne'er-do-well who ran with society's baser elements and happiest when sitting in front of a card table or throwing away money at the horse races. Alice was a decent woman from a respectable family and, by all rights, her path ought not to have ever crossed with such a man. There is no accounting for taste, however, and all it took was one look at him to set their short, sad story in motion.

Alice would have surely known that it did not befit her to associate with such a disreputable character, but, as far as she was concerned, she had no choice in the matter. To the horror of her family—and the collective joy of the area's chinwaggers—Alice began seeing this young man regularly. He came calling practically every day, weaseled his way onto invitation lists for almost every Bladensfield party and was frequently seen riding through the country with her.

As much as they liked one another, the couple faced one near-insurmountable obstacle to lasting happiness: Alice's scruples. Determined to protect her good name, she made it clear to her dubious suitor that she would not even consider marriage unless he changed his ways. Maybe such a condition would have been enough for this man to put his dissolute life behind him.

Or maybe not. No one would ever know for sure. Not long after meeting the man, Alice fell ill with an unknown illness that neither she nor Bladensfield would ever recover from. It happened during a trip to the mountains. She had departed vigorous and happy, the full blush of youth on her smiling face. When they brought her down from the mountain, she was nearly unrecognizable. Emaciated and pale as bone, she was unable to stay on her feet for more than a few minutes at a time.

Bedridden and getting worse by the day, she was slowly succumbing to the inevitable when her beau barged into the house and ran upstairs, where he fell at the bedside of the woman he loved. Alice managed a weak smile at the sight of him. He crawled up onto the bed with her, crying openly at her pallor and the way her skin stretched over the bones of her gaunt face. He leaned in to her, then, and told her what she had been waiting to hear for months. "I've changed," he said. "I've put my sinning ways behind me so I can be worthy."

Alice smiled at him, shaking her head gently; she had not heard what he said. So the man repeated himself: "I said it's over, Alice." His voice was urgent now. He needed for her to know. "I'm not gambling anymore. I don't go to the horse races either. You've reformed me. I'm a saved man."

But she was having trouble comprehending him on account of the spreading fever. Of course, she must have recognized the man, but it was as though she were in a dream. She reached up with a smile, pressing her cold palm against his face. And then she died, looking into his eyes, still smiling.

That was the last anyone saw of Westmoreland County's most popular misbehaver. He did not even wait to see Alice buried but rode out the very day she died without a word of farewell to anyone. Alice's death cast a long shadow over Bladensfield, and the succeeding days, weeks and months crept by for the Peck clan—quiet and joyless—while the ghosts of their stately old home started to stir.

Years passed. John Peck sold Bladensfield to Reverend Ward. The Civil War erupted with the hopes of Southern succession, and then ground to a bloody halt with the Confederacy's complete and utter defeat. The South tumbled into depression under the harsh rule of Reconstruction.

It was at this time that a stranger appeared at Bladensfield's door and introduced himself as Reverend Temple. He was an old man, though vigorous still, with bright blue eyes and an easy smile. His clothes were worn and muddy. A servant called for Mrs. Ward, who greeted the reverend with a smile.

"Greetings, ma'am," the reverend began. "I've been on the road for many miles, and would ask you to open your door to a man of God for one night only."

Mrs. Ward ushered the reverend in with a wide smile. "Of course, sir," she said, beaming, "our door is always open to the fine gentlemen of the South."

Crossing the threshold, the preacher seemed overtaken by a strange sensation. Tears began to form in his eyes, and he stopped for a moment, taking in the sight of the hall before him. "Why, Reverend," Mrs. Ward said, putting a steadying hand on his shoulder, "are you quite all right?" She stood and called for her daughter to fetch a glass of water, but the shaken old man stopped her.

"Thank you, ma'am, but that won't be necessary. Bit of a shock is all. I haven't been here for many years," he said.

Mrs. Ward was visibly surprised. "You know my home?"

"Yes, I do, ma'am. I used to visit here back when the Peck family owned it. Haven't been back around these parts for many years now." That was about as much as the reverend was willing to divulge. Mrs. Ward tried to ask him how he knew the Pecks, and what had brought him to her home so many years ago, but the reverend always shrugged and

*Who was this mysterious traveler to Bladensfield?*

changed the subject whenever Mrs. Ward brought up the past.

Mrs. Ward said nothing to the reverend, either, about all the stories circulating among the servants about the weird events that happened daily in her home. She did not approve of such nonsense, and forbid her children to repeat the tales: the legend of the exorcism that a Baptist preacher had attempted and the ghosts that continued to haunt anyway, the stern, angry apparition that was in the study and the beautiful apparition that was said to appear in one of the bedrooms on the second floor.

She tried to conceal her surprise when the reverend asked if he would be able to sleep in a particular room that night, if nobody else was using it.

"Well, of course, sir," Mrs. Ward replied. "No one has slept in that room for quite some time. You're more than welcome to sleep there." She said nothing about the ghost that was said to haunt it. After all, she had never seen the supposed apparition of Alice Peck in the bedroom. Besides, a person doesn't just bring up such things out of the blue, especially when talking to an ordained minister.

After dinner, Mrs. Ward led Reverend Temple to his room. She watched his reaction as she swung open the door and he looked inside for the first time. He flinched as though the sight of it was a blow. He seemed to regain his composure and, thanking Mrs. Ward for her hospitality, entered the bedroom and shut the door behind him.

The next morning, Reverend Temple was a different man. He was beaming as he came down the stairs and actually skipped as he approached the breakfast table. "Well, I say!"

Mrs. Ward declared after the preacher leapt into his chair. "Someone must have slept well last night!"

"I must correct you, ma'am," Reverend Temple said with a smile. "I did not sleep one minute in that room last night." He paused, remembering. "But I would not have missed it for anything."

A flicker of confusion played across Mrs. Ward's face. "But whatever do you mean, sir?"

He studied his hostess' face for a moment before he replied. "I only mean to say that it is good to be back here at Bladensfield. I have been reacquainted with some very old yet very dear memories. It was an experience that I will not soon forget."

An experience that he would not soon forget? And exactly what sort of experience was the reverend talking about, alone in a dark bedroom? Did he perhaps have a vivid dream that brought back fond memories of his youth? But hadn't he said he did not sleep at all? What, then, was this strange visitor talking about?

Maybe there was a moment, just a moment, when the story of Alice Peck flashed through Mrs. Ward's head. And perhaps, for that instant, she considered the possibility that Reverend Temple had encountered her much talked about apparition in the bedroom. But the reverend would say nothing that morning to shake her skepticism about the spirits that supposedly haunted her house.

Dodging Mrs. Ward's queries about what he had experienced in the room, Reverend Temple left shortly after breakfast, bestowing blessings with a grateful smile. Mounting his horse and riding off as quickly as he came, the old preacher never returned to Bladensfield.

Nevertheless, his visit would eventually become another page in the legend of Bladensfield. Servants who had overheard the exchange at the breakfast table spread word about the reverend's queer behavior. It was pretty well accepted that he had seen Alice Peck's ghost; all the signs were there. He wasn't the first to be overcome with a sense of euphoria after seeing the smiling apparition of the beautiful young woman. None of the servants doubted that Reverend Temple had seen her that night.

But it was the question of Reverend Temple's identity that got everyone talking. Who was this mysterious traveler, and why was it that he specifically requested to sleep in Alice Peck's old room, acknowledged as—besides John Peck's study—one of the two most haunted places in the house? Further, he had made it known that he had been a frequent visitor to Bladensfield years before. Maybe it says something about people's need to give their stories tidy endings, but it soon was accepted that Reverend Temple was none other than Alice's ne'er-do-well suitor, who had renounced his life of sin on her deathbed. He had devoted himself to the ministry, and only after a life of virtuous work did he feel worthy enough to revisit the place where his first and only love had lived and died. And he was only able to come to terms with his loss then, in his twilight years, after seeing Alice again as young and stunning as she was when he had known her.

So goes the story of Bladensfield. Time has not been so kind to the ghosts in this historic house, one of old Virginia's earliest homes. Tales of bizarre encounters within its walls have become less and less frequent over the years. Then again, who knows? This historic house has always been privately owned, not open to the prying eyes or overactive

imaginations of paranormal enthusiasts and curiosity seek-
ers. Perhaps all it would take to breathe new life into its legend is a single visit by a group of such individuals. So it's
probably for the best that Bladensfield remains undisturbed;
it isn't like the state of Virginia needs another addition to its
mile-long roster of haunted places.

# The Spirits in the Well

Josiah Deans removes a kerchief from his vest and wipes the sweat from his brow. "Bloody hot one," his overseer says, speaking loudly so as to be heard over the sounds of the slaves reaping the harvest. It is hot, but Deans says nothing, unable to voice any such complaint while he stands in a field of sweating men who have been toiling under the sun for most of the day. They sing as they labor, their voices carrying under the reddening sky, and they will still be heard well after the stars come out—there will be late work tonight, just as there was last night, the night before, and just as there will be for weeks to come.

It is the harvest of 1789, and Josiah Deans and his overseer are surveying the tortured gathering on Midlothian Plantation. Deans, striding through the middle of one of his cotton fields, hits his foot on something hard and stumbles. He almost pitches over it—a stone ring embedded in the ground, rising about a foot high, encircling a mound of earth and rocks. "Careful now." The overseer offers his boss an arm for support. Deans straightens himself, looks down and recognizes what is there.

"A well," he says.

"I'd say so, yeah," responds the overseer, who is also seeing it for the first time. "Filled in, though."

"I thought it odd when I bought this plantation," Deans continues, "that there was no field well."

"There it is," the overseer says. "Dare say it won't do anyone much good no more."

"That's the truth. But I wonder why it was filled in?" Only after these words are spoken do the planter and the overseer notice the silence. Off in the distance, the slaves' throaty singing continues, but those around the two men have become quiet. They are no longer working, either, but looking from the well to the two men to one another; a palpable uncertainty hangs in the sultry air. Deans is curious about this sudden interruption; the overseer sees disobedience and, naturally, potential danger.

He unfastens his whip from his belt. "An' what the hell you lot think you're doin'?" His voice is a jagged edge, promising violence. "Field ain't gonna harvest itself!" His other hand reaches for the pistol at his hip, and the men begin to turn back to their work.

"It's the well, sir." The words are heavy, but the field slave's voice is small, practically apologetic. Everyone stops and looks. The speaker steps forward—a bent old man with brilliant white hair and long muscular arms, glistening black in the day's last light. His heavy eyes bore straight through Josiah Deans. "They filled that there well in years back, when my ma was still a girl and they called this house the Middleway."

The overseer steps forward with a hard look, his pale hand raising the whip over his head. "You ain't here to give us no history lessons, old timer," he says. The old man bows his head, ready to receive the blow, but it never comes.

"Hold, sir," says Deans. "Let this man finish. He speaks of my property, and I wish to hear."

The old man raises his head, staring through the scowling face before him to a time when he was young and his hands were still unmarked by years of forced labor. He remembers standing where Deans stands now, listening to his mother telling him the story. "It was a preacher that did it," he begins. "A preacher man who chased two spirits into that there well and sealed it up behind them."

"A preacher chasin' two spirits into a well." The overseer tries to sneer, but he has obviously become uneasy. He knows little of the bizarre folk tales and mysterious rituals that often ring through the slave quarters after dark, but in the different plantations he has worked in he has seen enough to make him nervous whenever such topics come up.

"That he did," the old man says, staring down the overseer. "Had to. No choice, on account of them two refusin' to go under the ground on their own. They was buried good and proper, just like all the rest, but they didn't want to stay down there in the dirt. Preacher had to trick them to stay. And that's just what he did."

The congregation around the old man grows bigger as other slaves drop their work and gather around to hear the tale they have all heard many times before. Deans, as intrigued as they are, speaks next: "Who were these two men, then, who were buried but refused to stay there? And why would such souls rebel against the laws of God and nature and rise from the grave after death?"

"Not two men, sir," the old man replies. "One was a man, true enough—a young man they called Hubert, son of proud Mr. Iverson, master of the house. But the other," he pauses, addressing all before him now, "the other was a lady, a good and gentle lady they called Jennie Bower. All folks loved Jennie, but none more than Hubert. And she liked him back. They was sweet on each other, the way young people get. No one could keep them apart."

So begins the old man's story, the tragic tale of Hubert Iverson and Jenny Bower, which, in 1789, was already on its way to becoming a Gloucester County legend. The story took place in one of the region's oldest homes. Midlothian was a 1200-acre plantation that had come under the plough in the 17th century, when Virginia was still a colony whose loyal subjects had yet to dream of independence from the mother country.

Midlothian Plantation was then called Middleway, and the plantation founder was Mr. Iverson, who had a son named Hubert. Hubert was a good and honorable man by all accounts. There was no reason he would not have taken his father's place as Middleway's patriarch. Well, no reason besides Jennie Bower. She was the girl down the way, with bright rosy cheeks and strawberry curls, who was as poor as she was beautiful. Hubert fell in love with her. Neither her poverty nor his father's sanction meant anything to him. He had resolved to marry her, no matter what her social station, and that was that.

In the end, it was not his father's will that killed the union but an unknown fever, virulent and ultimately deadly, that claimed him before he was able to vow his devotion. He was not even able to see her as he lay dying, thanks to his father's stricture against her setting foot on his plantation. Still, Hubert saw his father regularly during his last days, and he would spend most of this time together trying to get his father to promise that he would look after Jennie and her family when Hubert was gone.

Mr. Iverson, however, was by this time a rather bitter man. Not only had his son—his pride and joy—decided to fall in love with a woman completely unbefitting his social status, but so, too, was this same son dying well before his time. He was in no mood to grant favors and vehemently promised his son that he would do no such thing. That, for as long as he lived, no Iverson would so much as lift a finger to provide for the Bower family. He promised this to his son, and then his son died. Not long after, so did Jennie, either of a broken heart or simple privation. Thus the last tragic word was written in yet another tale of star-crossed love.

But no, Jennie and Hubert were not quite ready to conclude their affair. Shortly after Jennie's death, all sorts of strange things began occurring in and around the great house. People sometimes heard the sound of moans in the hall in the middle of the night, and disembodied footsteps dragged themselves from room to room. At other times, people who thought they were alone would be startled half to death when someone, or something, let out a loud groan in an otherwise empty room or hallway. And these strange occurrences weren't all.

The Iversons and their servants regularly saw Jennie and Hubert in the house and the surrounding plantation. At times, they were seen reliving happier moments, embracing in the fields or walking hand in hand along the veranda at sunset. Other sightings were far less pleasant—like the one of young Jennie Bower, pale as the worn white dress hanging off her emaciated frame, wandering up to Hubert's old bedroom, an eerie expression on her dead face. Hubert was seen, too, often drifting down the main staircase, vanishing the moment he reached the ground floor, or else walking down the hall from his room to his father's in the middle of the night. More than once, Mr. Iverson woke to see the shimmering apparition of his dead son standing over his bed.

These continual reminders of the Iversons' loss were too much, and they eventually sold the plantation to the Marable family. The Iversons left Gloucester County for good, but the spirits of Jennie and Hubert stuck around, much to the Marables' eventual dismay.

It was essentially the same as it was with the previous owners—the mysterious noises in the middle of the night, the apparitions floating around the grounds and within the house.

"But them Marables, they was different from the Iverson folks," says the old man. "They was Christians, with real faith, and went to see a preacher about the spirits on the land. They didn't know young Mr. Iverson or Miz Bower, so their story didn't bother them none, they just wanted 'em gone, plain and simple."

The legend said nothing about whether or not Reverend Yates, the rector they approached about the problem, knew anything about what was going on, but he wasted no time confronting the two spirits.

"My ma was there the day the reverend came by to take care of business," says the old man. "It was right around sunset, and he called everyone out of the house, white and black folk alike, and went inside of there all by himself." Slaves working the field can still be heard singing around them, but everyone surrounding the old man is silent. Even the overseer is listening, his gaze shifting back and forth between the slave before him and the great house behind.

"And what did this Reverend Yates accomplish?" Deans finally asks. "He drew the spirits out, I suppose?"

"That he did, sir," the old man replies. "My ma told me that back in them days, preachers was of the belief that if a man wanted to take spirits out of his house, he had to walk backward while prayin.' Spirits would only follow a man if he was walkin' backward. That was the most important thing."

No one could have been too surprised, then, when Reverend Yates emerged from the house, solemnly going through a formal exorcism while walking backward, down the stairs and into the field slowly, one step at a time.

"He walked them two young folk right up to this well," the old man says, gesturing to the sealed spring before them. "With bell, book and candle he called them underneath, and they followed. Then he ordered, right then and there, that the well be sealed shut. My ma always told me that when they put the last rock down there, she heard a scream from down below, a scream of a real deep sadness, like from a young girl. And then that was it. No one saw or heard from Mr. Iverson or Miz Bower ever again."

The old man's story ends. Everyone is looking down at the sealed well in the fast-fading light of day. The slaves have heard this story before and generally avoid the well, just in case there is any truth to the old man's story. But this is the first time Josiah Deans and his overseer have heard it.

Finally, the overseer breaks the silence. "That it?" he snorts. "Two sweet young lovers in the bottom of this here well. That's gotta be the most foolish thing I've ever heard!" He lets out a loud laugh, but it's obviously forced, and Deans and the other men have difficulty joining in. Because there is something about the sight of this well, now. It could be the old man's story, or the way the deepening shadows play over the field, across the stone surface. No one feels like laughing.

Nevertheless, Deans knows full well what his overseer is doing. There's a lot of work to be done, and this little get-together in the middle of the field is eating into harvest time. "All right, men," he hollers, "story time's over. Let's get back to it."

The workers begin again, picking up their heavy tune as they reap another man's profit, and Deans and the overseer continue on their tour. Deans, a religious man, only ever brings up the field well once again, when he instructs the overseer that under no circumstances whatever is the well to be touched. If there really are two spirits residing in the bottom, it's best they stay there.

# The Wythe House

It was certainly an impressive dowry. Given by Richard Taliaferro to his daughter in 1775 when she married George Wythe, the stately brick dwelling was built for the burgeoning colonial elite. George Wythe could certainly count himself among them. America's first law professor, Wythe was instructor and mentor to none other than Thomas Jefferson, the luminary diplomat who, one year after Wythe moved into the house, helped draft the Declaration of Independence. In the years that followed, war between patriots and loyalists raged in the surrounding countryside. At one time during the campaign, George Washington and the Marquis de Lafayette used the George Wythe House for their temporary headquarters. After independence, the building stood through the golden age of the plantation culture, the Civil War, the brutal years of Reconstruction, continued economic depression and then a slow, plodding recovery.

"If these walls could speak" goes the old saying, and at the George Wythe House some might say that they do. Then again, often there are other people doing the speaking for them. The George Wythe House is part of the Williamsburg Colonial Village, a living museum in the heart of Williamsburg, where visitors can explore the region's past in 160 buildings and historical reenactments that occur throughout the complex. As well, costumed interpreters give guided tours through some of the buildings, and the George Wythe House's history is regularly recounted. In a place so conscious of its own history, the story of George Wythe

House has been well documented and is constantly told and retold to visitors.

Historical interpreters aren't the only ones keeping the past alive at George Wythe House. For as long as anyone can remember, there have been strange activities at the old colonial pile, bizarre phenomena that are popularly attributed to the building's most infamous one-time resident—Lady Ann Skipwith.

As is often the case when legend blurs with history, the facts of Ann Skipwith's life differ depending on who's telling the story. What is generally agreed upon is that she was married to Sir Peyton Skipwith, and the couple were friends with the Wythes. Through much of the late 1770s, the Skipwiths regularly enjoyed extended stays at the George Wythe House—until 1779, when Lady Ann Skipwith died.

She was buried in the graveyard of nearby Bruton Parish Church. The weird occurrences at the George Wythe House began almost as soon as she was laid in the ground. It did not take long after that for people to begin talking about the circumstances behind the young woman's death. There were two versions that stuck. In one, Ann Skipwith died of a miscarriage, breathing her last in the arms of her wailing husband. The other, though no less tragic, presents a much darker view of the Skipwiths' relationship. Peyton Skipwith is cast as an inveterate womanizer, and Ann Skipwith as the angry and humiliated wife. According to this version, Ann Skipwith simply reached the breaking point with her husband's philandering, and, perceiving no honorable options available to her in the traditional culture of the antebellum South, committed suicide.

Choose whichever version of the story you like. But if ghostly activity is a spiritual residue left behind in the wake of exceptionally tragic or traumatic events, then either variation of Ann Skipwith's demise is tragic and traumatic enough to qualify as an explanation for the things that are said to go on at the George Wythe House. Whatever the circumstances of her demise, some part of Lady Ann has remained behind in the old Williamsburg home—she is assumed to be the woman in the closet.

If the stories are to be believed, she has been sighted countless times over the years—a beautiful woman dressed resplendently in a ball gown about 200 years out of fashion. It is always the same. The closet in her former bedroom swings open, and the room is suddenly filled with the scent of lavender. Out she comes, all ready for a colonial ball in her cream-colored satin dress, her bright red shoes barely visible beneath the hem of her gown. She moves stiffly, stepping out of the closet and turning as the door shuts behind her. Then she turns an expressionless gaze into the mirror, staring, trance-like, at her reflection before abruptly vanishing, never so much as acknowledging startled visitors.

The same overdressed woman has been spotted in other parts of the house. More than one report has her appearing on the stairs in the same satin dress, though this time her dress is pulled up slightly, and it is clear that she is wearing only one red shoe while the other stocking-clad foot is shoeless. These sightings are believed to correspond with another fairly common incident said to occur in the house, where the sound of lopsided footfalls is heard going up the stairs, although there is no one there. The footsteps are usually described as uneven—alternating between a sharp clack, like the sound of the heel of a shoe on the stairs, and a dull thud, as though the other foot is unshod. Thus the invisible presence is deemed to have on only one shoe, like the woman whom others have seen standing impassive on the stairs.

Anyone wondering what a woman in a ball gown is doing running up and down the stairs with one shoe on might be interested in consulting the local folklore. There is a tale concerning Ann Skipwith and her husband at a ball at the governor's palace. Peyton Skipwith showed up at the ball, as the story goes, with Lady Ann on his arm. The couple danced a few minuets and made their rounds of the room, but it was not long before Skipwith's eye began to wander. While Lady Ann continued to make small talk with her acquaintances, her husband left her side to strike up a conversation with another woman. Incredulous, Lady Ann watched as her husband paid the other woman an improper amount of attention.

Wavering between jealously, rage and humiliation, Lady Ann fled the ballroom, slowing only upon reaching the front door when she heard her husband calling her name. He was apparently making an attempt at conciliation, but she was too consumed by her voluminous rage to pay any attention to him. Skipwith, deciding that the foyer of the governor's palace was not the best place to air their domestic disputes, turned his back to his wife and returned to the party. Lady Ann stormed to her carriage. In her rush, she lost one of her shoes while stepping up to her carriage, but she was so upset that she did not retrieve it. She arrived at the George Wythe House with only one shoe on, and promptly ran up the stairs to her room and slammed the door shut behind her.

Among those who believe that Ann Skipwith committed suicide, it is said that she took her life soon after—if not on this very night, then at some point over the next few days. Whether she took her life or not, the events of that evening were certainly traumatic enough for her spirit to continue reliving them centuries after she passed. Lady Ann's furious flight from the governor's ball may explain the lopsided footfalls and appearance of the one-shoed phantom, but there is also another spirit that is said to haunt the historic home— that of George Wythe himself.

Ann Skipwith was not the only historic resident of the Williamsburg home to suffer an untimely death. In Wythe's case, it was his standing as one of Virginia's wealthiest citizens that led to his demise. Having moved to Richmond in 1791 to become Virginia's chancellor, Wythe had been living in the state capital for over a decade when, in 1806, he fell dreadfully ill. It was no natural illness; the old man was poisoned by his grandnephew, George Sweeney, who was also the principal beneficiary of Wythe's will. Sweeney, heavily in debt and on the brink of destitution, was all too willing to expedite his inheritance but was ultimately foiled. Though George Wythe was almost 80 when he unknowingly imbibed his treacherous grandnephew's toxin, he did not die immediately. He continued to draw breath for another two weeks, lying in an agonized state of near-death, cursing the man who had inflicted such suffering upon him. In that time, it came to light that the culprit was none other than his grandnephew. Before succumbing to death on June 8, 1806, Wythe's last act was to remove Sweeney from his will.

George Wythe did not die in his house, but some people believe that his spirit returned afterward, if not to reside there then at least to visit every year on the day of his death. The legend tells us that anyone sleeping in the former chancellor's bedroom on that date will be woken in the middle of the night by an icy hand pressed palm down against his forehead. The victim's reaction is always the same—the shout, the jump from the bed, the hands reaching for the light. And then the chilling silence, the bafflement. For it is clear by the light from the bedside lamp: the room is empty, without a trace of anyone having been there—except, that is, the feeling of that hand on the forehead, the skin still tingling at the icy memory.

There have been various theories about the recurring phenomenon in Wythe's bedroom. Although it is generally agreed that the invisible hand must belong to old George Wythe himself, there is no way of knowing for certain because no one has actually seen him. Still, if it is the spirit of George Wythe, why does he haunt the Williamsburg house, nearly 50 miles away from Richmond, where he died? Is he upset that others have been sleeping in his old room? Given his habit of waking individuals sleeping in his bed by pressing an ice-cold hand against their foreheads, it would certainly seem so. But then, why does he only present himself one day of the year? And why does he limit his activity to such an innocuous, if admittedly creepy, action?

As is so often the case where paranormal phenomena are concerned, these questions are likely to go unanswered. Given the persistence of the spirits of George Wythe and Lady Ann Skipwith over the last two centuries, they will likely continue to lurk in the darkness of the George Wythe House for years to come.

# The Hanging Pirates
# of Gallows Road

*The Seas are soe full of Pyrates that it is almost impossible
for any ships to goe home to England in safety.*

—William Berkeley, Governor of Virginia, 1660

He was born into the world as Edward Teach, but his calling to murder and villainy on the clear blue waters between the New World and the old branded him with another name. From anonymous provenance in Bristol, England, Teach sailed to the West Indies as a merchant seaman. War with the French turned him from a merchant to a privateer, and it was while he was on board a vessel preying on French ships in the Caribbean that he discovered his natural talent for violence. Yet when the war with the French ended, Teach was suddenly deprived of an outlet for this talent and so pursued what he saw as the only other option for a rum-loving, cutlass-swinging sea dog such as himself.

In the port of New Providence, in the Bahamas, he signed on as a crewman of a pirate ship and never looked back. Sailing under the Jolly Roger, he went across the Caribbean from Jamaica to Barbados, Bermuda to Trinidad. He zealously participated in the raids, indiscriminately going after French, English and Spanish vessels alike, as long as the Jolly Roger was the ship with more guns.

From the beginning, he stood out as particularly gifted at this line of work—the most fearsome fighter, the most fervent drinker, the most cunning sailor. He advanced quickly in the rough hierarchy of pirates and was soon a captain himself, mercilessly commandeering his own vessel. It was while he was captain of the *Queen Anne's Revenge,* with 40 cannons at the gun ports and the ugliest crew in the West Indies, that Edward Teach began making his place in history.

Routinely overrunning the fully manned warships of Britain's Royal Navy, he earned a reputation for unparalleled ferociousness. None who saw him storming up and down his deck, bellowing orders and obscenities, forgot the sight. A giant of a man with thick shoulders and a heavy stride, he wore a bandolier stuffed with six single-shot pistols and as many daggers, and a heavy cutlass hung from his side. He plaited his coal black beard with colorful ribbons. If he was going into battle, he would tie long, slow-burning candle wicks into the broad tresses so that thick tendrils of smoke curled around his face. He was transformed on those waters from Edward Teach to the dreaded pirate Blackbeard. His name became known in every port from the Caribbean to Chesapeake Bay and beyond.

No one was safe. Blackbeard roamed far and wide, his plundering taking him from warm Caribbean waters up the Atlantic coast to the colonies of Virginia, North Carolina and as far north as Pennsylvania. Seaborne trade between Europe and the colonies was abundant, and there was a fortune to be had for those with the necessary gumption, sea legs and scarcity of scruples required to hijack the wealth of powerful men.

Blackbeard was so good at it that he was eventually able to buy himself some measure of respectability. "Respectability" might sound like the wrong word for a man who made a practice of tying burning matches into his beard and robbing at cutlass point, but it shows that anything is available to you if you have enough money to buy it. In 1717, he approached Governor Charles Eden of North Carolina and, along with 20 of his men, received the King's pardon for all the crimes of which he had been accused.

Settling into the colony, Blackbeard moved into a stately home near the town of Bath, North Carolina, and promptly set about impressing his well-heeled neighbors with his ostentatious parties and limitless supplies of fine rum. He even went ahead and got married—to his 14th wife. Maybe, this time around, the pirate intended to make a go of it. Well, on the one hand there were such fine intentions, and on the other was the call of the open sea. The intentions were quickly forgotten. Plaiting his beard and strapping on his bandolier, Blackbeard resumed his life of cutthroat piracy, striking at the money-laden ships off the Atlantic coast with remarkable ferocity. Word spread quickly. Blackbeard was back.

The merchants sailing out of Virginia and North Carolina were most aware of his return. Blackbeard seemed to develop a certain fondness for Chesapeake Bay, patrolling the sea lanes and hitting merchant ships before they were even able to make it out to the Atlantic. The fact that the nefarious pirate had cultivated something of a working relationship with North Carolina's governor probably made him feel a sense of entitlement over these waters. He certainly plundered as though it was his domain. Chesapeake Bay became such a hornet's nest of piracy that skittish captains were more and more reluctant to leave the safety of their ports. There was one six-week period during which not a single ship left Virginia's ports.

In the end, it was a formal plea from a group of North Carolina merchants that impelled Virginia's governor, Alexander Spotswood, to act. He commissioned Lieutenant Robert Maynard to go after the legendary pirate. On November 17, 1717, with two fast sloops under his command, Maynard pulled out of Chesapeake Bay, bound for Blackbeard's rumored hideout near Ocracoke Island off North Carolina's Outer Banks.

Five days later, in the open water of Ocracoke Inlet, Maynard was standing on the deck of his ship, his telescope trained on a vessel approaching fast. From its topmast it was flying a flag of a horned skull—Blackbeard's insignia. Then the dreaded pirate himself was visible in the telescope: a giant, bristling with weapons, his beard tied with colorful ribbons and emitting heavy wafts of black smoke. Striding back and forth across his ship, he was roaring orders. They were coming up fast and would be on him and his crew, Maynard knew, in a matter of minutes.

The lieutenant acted fast, ordering his marines to fire a volley from their muskets before taking cover below deck, so that his ship would appear to be undermanned. Maynard would later write that when Blackbeard's men fired back, he could hear the fearsome pirate captain over the din, roaring curses and contempt at his opponents, swearing that he would not ask for quarter, nor would any be granted.

The pirates boarded quickly, confidently swinging up on the British vessel, sure that strength of numbers was on their side. Then Maynard gave the word, and the British rushed up, falling upon the pirates from all sides with musket, cutlass and pistol. Blackbeard was in the midst of it, sweeping over the ship with cutlass in one hand, pistol in

*Despite his violent death, Blackbeard never joined his phantom crew on Gallows Road.*

the other, cutting apart his enemies as he went. He fought until he emptied every gun in his bandolier, until all his daggers were lost in the bodies of his foes, until all he had was his cutlass, covered to the hilt in blood. And then he fought on. He was slashed across the chest, stabbed in the arm, shot through the face. The soldier who embedded his cutlass in Blackbeard's leg lost his head an instant later. The man who left his dagger protruding from the pirate's back had an arm severed for his troubles. Covered in his own blood and the blood of others, bellowing every obscenity in his prodigiously obscene vocabulary, Blackbeard cut a line to Maynard. On his way, a broad-shouldered Scot landed a fatal blow with his sword, thus ending the life of the legendary pirate. Almost the moment Blackbeard fell, those men under his command gave up their arms. In that one battle, he had been shot five times and stabbed over 20 before he and his scoundrels had been defeated.

There would be more depravities on Ocracoke Inlet that day. Ordering the 15 captured pirates to be locked in the brig, Maynard promptly beheaded Blackbeard and had the pirate's head hoisted up on the bowsprit. Then he had the pirate's body dumped into the bloodied waters around his ship. The impression the pirate had made was such that a few of the sailors present swore his headless body swam once around the sloop before it sank to the bottom.

Maynard returned to Virginia victorious. The lieutenant collected his reward, while his gruesome trophy was mounted high over the entrance to the Hampton River, where it served as a warning for many years. The spot was later called Blackbeard's Point—a reminder to everyone of the fate of those who dared sail under the Jolly Roger.

Contrary to what some might expect, there is no legend of a headless Edward Teach in the annals of Virginia's folklore. There is one popular story that has Blackbeard's skull finally being removed from where it was displayed and then fixed into the base of an ornate punch bowl. A variation of this tale has the skull lined with silver and made into a goblet. But surprisingly there have been no accounts of Edward Teach returning from his watery grave to punish those who so mutilated his remains.

Not so of the pirates who served under him, however. Of the 15 men who were captured that bloody November day, 13 were condemned to death. They were hanged in springtime the following year. Taken from Williamsburg's public jail, they were carted atop their own coffins to Gallows Road, where before a crowd of spectators they were read their crimes and then hanged.

There are some paranormal enthusiasts who believe that something of these men has remained behind. Soon after these pirates were put to death, people began talking of strange noises in the middle of the night. Certain individuals walking along Gallows Road claimed to hear carts rumbling by in the darkness, though there were no carts to be seen. Others spoke of the sound of straining gallows followed by long, agonized moans. Of course, people linked these to Blackbeard's pirates and took to avoiding Gallows Road after the sun went down.

Nearly three centuries later, Gallows Road in Williamsburg has long since been renamed Capitol Landing Road, and colonial Williamsburg stands anachronistically amid the trappings and technology of the 21st century. Yet some might say that this does not matter at all to the seafaring men who, once upon a time, had their necks stretched there. To this day, some people claim to hear the wheels of the phantom carts rumbling down the lane and the agonized moans of the 13 dead pirates.

# The Thing that Happened in the Town of Buchanan

*For five days during the past week the manifestations were frequent, varied and violent. Brickbats, old bones, billets of wood, ears of corn, stones, etc., were thrown about the house in the most unaccountable manner, and again and again everything would be turned topsy-turvy in the parlour and the chambers without their being able to detect the agent.*

—Excerpt from a letter from Reverend G.C. Thrasher to the *Lexington Gazette*, November 1870

It began harmlessly enough. Reverend Thrasher, a Baptist minister living in the small town of Buchanan, Botetourt County, woke from his bed, put on some clothes and went to the kitchen, where he lit a fire in the stove and placed a pot of water on top. He looked out the window into his yard. A sack of corn he had recently purchased was lying there by his gate, about 20 yards from the bin he had stored it in two days before. The sack had been cut open, its contents emptied all over his property.

Grumbling to himself about adolescents and their need for lawlessness, he trudged out into his yard and slowly retrieved the corn. His sack full, he walked over to the storage bin. He froze—the bin was still padlocked. *How did they get into the bin without breaking the lock?* he asked himself. He stared down at the sack of corn in his hands. *Is this is not my corn?*

He put his key into the lock and opened the bin. It was definitely his corn. Whoever performed this magic trick had indeed emptied the grain all over the yard. How it was done without breaking the lock or the bin, however, was a mystery. *Picked the lock, perhaps?* But that would mean there was a lock-picker in his small, rural town, where everyone knew everyone. He was aware of no one in Buchanan with such talents.

The hiss of water boiling over onto his stove snapped him out of his musings. Uttering a few more oaths about the mischief of youth, he ran back into his house to take the water off the fire. Reverend Thrasher did not think about the sack of corn again, not realizing that similar events were about to turn his life into chaos.

Over the next few days, his home seemed to acquire a mysterious habit of its own. Starting on the same day he found the corn scattered over his yard, things got progressively crazier. He went for a walk after having his coffee and breakfast one morning. When he returned, he found every window of his house, each of which had been locked from the inside, open. Assuming his three sons were in the midst of some foolish game, he ran into his house to scold them about leaving the place so open—only to discover his sons were still sleeping. *Impossible*, he told himself. *Who do they think I am, horsing around like this?*

He shook them awake, demanding that they go lock all the windows they had opened, and telling them he would not tolerate such nonsense in his house. He stuck to his guns despite their protests of innocence. They had been sleeping the whole time, they said. How was it possible they opened the windows?

"What, then," came Reverend Thrasher's response, "did the house do it on its own?" If only he knew how prescient this statement was.

With each passing day there were stranger and stranger occurrences in and around the house. Being a rationally minded man, Reverend Thrasher attributed the cause of these occurrences to his sons and his servant girl for as long as he was able. When a harsh rapping at his door interrupted his sermon writing and he opened the door to find no one there, he blamed his fastest son for playing such a senseless prank and punished the boy with extra chores. When he walked into his kitchen to find every piece of cookware he owned scattered all over floor, his chairs knocked over and his knives embedded in the walls, he roared at his servant, daring her to try such misbehavior again. He promised the tearful girl that if she did, the loss of her job would be the least of her concerns. And so it continued: doors he left unlocked just minutes before were locked when he returned to them, while doors and windows he locked developed a habit of unlocking almost the instant he turned his back. Twice, after leaving to run errands, he returned to find that every piece of furniture he owned had been rearranged.

Reverend Thrasher continued to place the blame on others, though it was getting harder and harder to do. Then, when he was sitting in the kitchen for lunch, three knives picked themselves up off of the table, went flying across the room and embedded themselves in the wall by the door. He was a man who had always taken pride in his logical disposition. He then knew what he had just witnessed defied all reasonable explanation, and that all the shouting and blame he had dispensed to his sons and his servant was misguided.

Something else was at work in his home. The preacher in him woke up, and he thought—*something evil.*

Succumbing to a numbing terror, Reverend Thrasher got up to leave but found the door was locked, even though he knew it had been unlocked mere minutes ago. He went to his room to retrieve his keys and discovered that, while he was in the kitchen, his bed had been noiselessly turned upside down; the frame was resting on the mattress, which was pressed against the floor. Just then, a deafening banging on his door made him jump. He ran to the door, pulled out his key but found that it was now unlocked. By the time he opened the door, his hands were trembling violently. Of course, there was nobody there. Five days later, he wrote his letter to the *Lexington Gazette* in which he described in great detail the phenomena occurring in his home.

The year was 1870, the month, November, and the infamous haunting of the Thrasher house was just getting started—a four-month period of intense poltergeist activity that ultimately culminated with Reverend Thrasher's surrendering his home and moving to Tennessee. But he did not go without a fight.

One of the first things the reverend did, after he recognized he was up against forces bigger than he, was go to the community for help. No one knows what words he used to recruit that first group of men to his aid, but they came and stood a vigilant watch over his home that night. It was hoped that if they kept their eyes open, these men might be able to determine a cause or a culprit. The reasoning was that there must be some agent responsible, something must have changed in the last few days to bring this otherworldly fury down upon Reverend Thrasher's house. Was there a witch? Had someone uttered a curse? Had anyone placed evil symbols in or around his home?

They kept their eyes open throughout the night and into the day but discovered no obvious cause for the anomalies. There was plenty of effect, however. Anyone who spent any amount of time in that house during those four months would, more often than not, leave awestruck at what had been seen within.

It was chaos unleashed at all hours. Men who took guard duty inside the house often found themselves dodging flying knives, forks, chairs and tables. The heaviest household items were regularly picked up and tossed as though they were toys. As Reverend Thrasher himself already had discovered, doors and windows would lock and unlock on their own. Sometimes, the furniture would not be sent crashing but would be rear-ranged impossibly fast and in gravity-defying patterns. For example, a guard watching over the parlor left it looking in order. When he returned not a minute later, he found the couch balanced precariously on one leg, supporting the arm-chair and the coffee table on its highest armrest, while one of the bookshelves jutted out, horizontal to the ground from its center. This impossible arrangement lasted just long enough for the bewildered guard to see; then it came crashing down in a heap. On other nights, there was such heavy pounding on the walls of the house that the door rattled on its hinges and the building's very foundations shook.

All the while, the surrounding area was as peaceful as ever. A person walking by the Thrasher house would scarcely notice anything was wrong. And, search as they did, no one found any trace of a hex or curse on the house. There were no dead rats pinned into the center of pentagrams, no black cats watch-ing intently from the bushes—nothing at all that suggested any sort of evildoing. Everyone, including Reverend Thrasher, was at a complete loss. One day, everything about the house was fine; then, out of nowhere, it was possessed. But by what?

Reverend Thrasher was trying to figure it all out when he sought out the aid of two early paranormal investigators. They were two young women, ardent spiritualists who were caught up in the paranormal movement that was sweeping the country at the time. They told Reverend Thrasher that they had sat in on countless séances, and the realm of the dead did not frighten them. They had wandered those gray lands before. It should be remembered that the reverend was not only a man of logical leanings but also a man of God, and it would surely have offended his sensibilities, resorting to the aid of these two women. But, by this point, he was desperate and ready to try anything.

The women were methodical in their approach. Set on getting to the bottom of the mystery, they went through the entire house. They put all of Thrasher's possessions in careful order, locked every door and took notes of where everything was and how it was placed. They hoped to be able to glean some answers from the way everything would be cast into disorder. Exiting the house, then, they noted the exact time they waited outside before going back in. Even their prodigious experience in such matters did not prepare them for what they saw inside.

The following are Reverend Thrasher's words:

> …the doors have been opened, the books from the center table scattered over the floor, the lamps from the mantelpiece put on the ground, and things disarranged generally; and, to increase the mystery, they found a strange key that would neither unlock nor lock any door in the house, sticking in the keyhole of the parlor door.

Overwhelmed by the scope of the disorder and bewildered by the appearance of this key, the two women were unable to offer any help at all, and they left.

Reverend Thrasher decided there was nothing he could do. His house had been taken over by some evil force he could never hope to understand. It took him four months to accept this decision, but as soon as he did, he acted. He and his family abandoned their home and moved far away, to Tennessee, where they prayed every day that the evil would not follow them.

As it turned out, the mysterious evil left before they did. Exactly one week before the Thrashers were to go, the destruction stopped. The violent and terrible forces that controlled the house for so long went still. The guards went home, and the reverend and his family were able to sleep peacefully once again.

But they did not change their plans. The family moved west. They built a new home and prospered peacefully. Maybe the prayers worked. As for the house in Buchanan, it is likely that no one will ever know what happened. To this day, the things that transpired in that western Virginia home and why they occurred remain among Botetourt County's greatest mysteries.

# Nell's Creek

There was a time when oyster men could be found on the waters of Nell's Creek. In the mornings they headed for the rich oyster beds on the James River. In the evenings they anchored their vessels near the mouth of the creek, where they congregated over oyster shells and alcohol. They counted their catch, told stories, sang songs. From the tributaries of the James, they came—from Deep Creek, Lucas Creek, Warwick River—weighing anchor in a sheltered cove where Nell's Creek emptied into the James. Always there would be at least one other boat with booze and cards and ready laughter. They were nothing less than a community, this rough fraternity of oyster men with their own argot, their own values and, of course, their own myths. The tale of willful and passionate Nell, from whom the creek took its name, was the one they knew best.

According to the legend, Nell was a beautiful, young woman from a family of some standing. Her problem was twofold: she had an independent nature and a fiery temperament. These traits did not do much for her relationship with her father, a man who believed that women ought to be obedient and submissive, passed on from their father's ownership to their husband's (assuming, of course, that the father approved of the union). Sadly, this state of affairs would not be the case with Nell.

She met him on the bank of the James. An oyster man, he had no prestigious family name or great wealth—he was happy living day to day, getting what he needed from the river. This lifestyle did not stop Nell from falling for him. She took to escaping every day from the stern gaze of her father and into the arms of the oyster man. Their attraction was mutual. They soon made vows to marry, and Nell, knowing her father would never allow it, told her fiancé that getting married would also mean running away, leaving the James River behind. Her lover was not bothered by this hitch; he owned nothing but his boat and could make a living wherever there was water.

So it was set: they were to be married right after Nell told her father of her intention. Impossible as he was, he was still her father, and Nell thought he deserved to know what she was going to do. She had no intention of asking for his blessing, but she would not leave without at least saying goodbye.

She took her fiancé with her so her father would be able to see the man she was planning to marry. His reaction did not surprise her. He was angry enough to learn that she had been seeing a suitor without his knowledge or permission, but one look at the young man's tattered clothing and unkempt hair, and he flew into a rage. His daughter had fallen in love with *this* man? Impossible.

He forbade it. Without hearing a word the young man had to say, Nell's father had him thrown out of his house. Nell protested violently, railing against her father. He responded by dragging her up to her room and locking her inside. She continued to shout through the door, telling him that there was nothing he could do, that she was going to get married regardless of what he thought.

That was when Nell's father uttered his terrible vow. "I swear to you, daughter," he said, "if you go ahead and marry that man against my will, I will kill you and bury you in the ground with your dowry. This, I promise."

She heard the threat in her father's voice. She knew he meant his words, and yet all they did was strengthen her resolve. Running away at the first chance she got, she met her oyster man by the James, and they went together to be married in secret by a local preacher. That night, they made plans to run off and start a new life somewhere else. But they did not make it.

When Nell's father discovered she had gone, he was beside himself with rage. He did not waste a moment but armed himself, saddled his horse and set out to look for his recalcitrant child. It is not known what transpired between the two when he found her. Was there a struggle? A discussion? Did her father attempt to bully Nell into coming back with him? Or did he make good on his promise in grim silence? And where was Nell's husband? No one can say. What is known is the ultimate outcome of that meeting. As he had sworn, Nell's father killed her and buried her along with the generous dowry she would have received had she married someone he approved of.

That was the end of Nell's life but just the beginning of the tale. It is a tale that defies any kind of solid timeline. Nell's date of birth is not known; neither is her age when she met her James River oyster man nor the year her father killed her. Likewise, although it is largely believed that the bizarre visitations on oyster men's boats on the James began sometime in the late 19th century, it is not known how much time had elapsed between her death and the earliest reports. Did she begin visiting boats up and down the James River the moment her father took her life, or did it take a while? Whatever the case, while the oyster men were there, so was the phantom of poor Nell.

Her tale was tragic, but Nell herself was a remarkably content spirit without a trace of ill will or vengefulness toward those she visited. Boatmen always welcomed her arrival on their vessels. She became something of an honorary oyster man herself, keeping lonely boatmen company, informing others who were down on their luck where the most plentiful beds were that day, even occasionally passing messages between the boats.

At first, it must have been difficult to figure out because Nell never appeared as an apparition. Rather, her spirit was an auditory manifestation; oyster men came to recognize she was there by the rapping on the cabin roofs of their boats. When Nell began to haunt the river, the oyster men would surely have been puzzled by the knocking on the tops of their boats, especially when an investigation always revealed that there was no one there.

It probably took a long time and many conversations among the oyster men, but eventually someone must have suggested that something might be doing the knocking, and then got the idea of attempting to communicate. Not long after that first hello, Nell's story began to emerge. The oyster men developed a system of communication that was very similar to the way some psychics at the time had been purportedly speaking with the dead. Since Nell's spirit was not able to speak, they codified knocking patterns into specific words. One knock meant yes, two knocks was no. If she wanted to spell something out, she would produce a succession of raps, the number of knocks corresponding to where the letter fell in the alphabet.

This was how the oyster men got to know Nell, who always announced her arrival with a lively rapping on the cabin roof. In L.B. Taylor's book *The Ghosts of Virginia*, an elderly man known only as J.P. recalls his experiences with Nell back when there were still oyster men on Nell's Creek.

Speaking of the first time he heard Nell knocking, the old boatman says: "I guess I was 18 or 20 when I experienced it. We were laid up overnight in the cove and I was standing outside the cabin with my head tucked inside, listening to the conversation. The cabin was full of watermen talking. There was a very distinct knocking on top of the cabin. When I poked my head outside, it sounded like it came from inside. And when I ducked my head inside the cabin, it sounded like it came from the outside. There was no way it could have been a hoax. I wasn't really scared, but I must have looked concerned because someone laughed and said, 'That's just ol' Nell.'"

Once an oyster man got used to Nell's visitations, she could be very useful informing a man how many oysters others were catching in different areas of the river. And her knowledge was not limited to the James River—far from it. Nell's ghost had an uncanny way of knowing almost everything. J.P. states: "She could answer anything she was asked. You could ask her how many children someone had, and she would rap out the numbers in knocks on the cabin. You could ask her someone's age and she knew it exactly. My father said one time a man grabbed a handful of beans out of a sack and asked her how many he had. She told him, to the bean!"

Yet she would not play along with all of the oyster men's questions. She was generally open with the men on the river, but every now and then one of these rough men would ask her a question that would offend her. When this happened, she was not above rocking their boats. She stirred the waters

*Boatmen always welcomed Nell on their vessels.*

of the James until they roiled violently around the vessel, making it pitch to and fro until the offending waterman took back whatever he had said.

Although Nell was not so easy to offend, according to legend, there was one thing she could not abide—the Holy Bible. Or, perhaps more accurately, the book of Deuteronomy, which is where the Ten Commandments were written. According to J.P., his brother, a religious man, took the Bible out onto the river once. Having weighed in for the night, he was reading from it when he heard Nell herald her arrival with a series of knocks on his roof. He welcomed the friendly spirit to his boat, and began reading out loud for her benefit.

Nell wanted none of it. As soon as he began reading, she responded with a continuous knocking. He continued, but the knocking grew louder, and so hard that for a second he feared she might damage his ship. He stopped reading, and as soon as he did, so, too, did Nell fall silent. There was no response when he asked her why she had gotten so upset. He waited and asked again, but the only sound was the water lapping upon the ship. Nell was gone. She did not return again for the rest of the night.

He was trying to figure out what issue Nell could have with the Bible when he remembered how she had died; her father had murdered her. J.P.'s brother had been reading from Deuteronomy, right before the Ten Commandments, the fifth and sixth of which famously read: "Honor thy father and thy mother," and "Thou shall not kill."

Even though the James' oyster men knew Nell's story, they were short on specifics. Nell never revealed what town she was from, what her last name was or the name of her husband. But, most importantly, as far as the river men were concerned, she did not say where she had been buried. Occasionally, someone would lament this fact, insisting that a woman of Nell's character deserved a proper burial, but everyone knew what this individual was *really* saying—where Nell's remains lay, there, too, did her dowry, and a rich one at that.

More than one man went looking for Nell's treasure, hoping to strike it rich somewhere around the creek that bears her name, but nothing has ever been found. Some people have said that there were strong supernatural forces working against those who went looking, such as sudden storms so fierce that they forced men to turn back and swarms of hornets and of wasps that descended on eager diggers. It was eventually decided that Nell's treasure belonged to Nell alone and was best left undisturbed.

It is doubtful that this resolution would have stuck if the government had not taken over all the land surrounding Fort Eustis in the 1930s, effectively ending the oyster men's forays onto the land around Nell's Creek. After that, the oyster men's ally stopped drifting over the James River, and no one heard her knocking again. Where did she go? Maybe she did not like the military. Maybe someone ran off with her treasure, and she went off in pursuit. Or maybe she finally forgave her father, and her spirit was allowed to rest. Then again, most of the oyster men she entertained have passed on themselves. Perhaps they continue to spend their time with Nell along oyster beds in some other place.

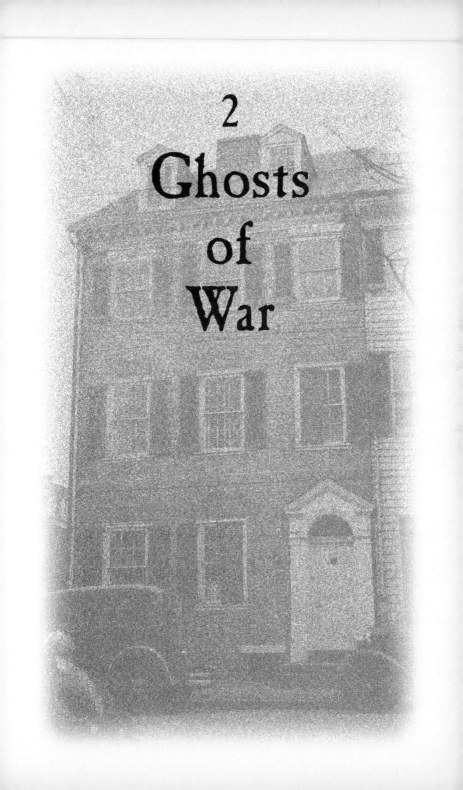

2

# Ghosts
# of
# War

# The Spy

John Dixon stood before the firing squad, staring down a row of rifle barrels. The Revolutionary War was raging, and he had been accused of the greatest crime in the colonies—collaboration with the Revolutionary forces. Weeks before, he had been dragged into a courthouse and made to hear the indictment against him. "The accused is a spy," read the charge. "He has been reporting crucial information to seditious subjects of the Crown and will be tried as a traitor to the colony of Virginia."

Along with so many others who were accused of joining the wrong side during America's early years, John Dixon was found guilty of being a spy and given the death sentence. As it turned out, however, he would also end up being a victim of judicial error. Dixon was innocent, but it would not become known until after he had been shot to death by a line of British soldiers.

The ugly little incident was quickly swept away by larger historical events. War is a brutal business, after all, composed of thousands of unseen tragedies. When it comes to war, human memory is inclined to dwell on the handful of resulting *events* rather than the myriad deaths involved in them— the Revolutionary forces drive the British from Yorktown, a peace treaty is signed, George Washington is the first president of the United States. The story of one man dying in a time when death was reaping a lush harvest could be easily forgotten. Indeed, where does one man's unjust end fit into such broad, historical currents?

Time has all but forgotten John Dixon, whose unfortunate fate has entered the realm of folklore. If his ghost wasn't haunting his former home in Alexandria's Old Town, it is certain he would have been forgotten altogether. But his story has survived, largely on account of his resentful spirit.

If, as many paranormal enthusiasts will state, ghosts are spirits unable to "move on" because of tragedy or trauma suffered while they were alive, then it is easy to understand why there is a ghost of John Dixon in the first place. Who can say what he was thinking during his final moments? It would not just be his terror or rage at the wrongful execution. He had no way of knowing he would be found innocent after he was killed, so in his eyes it was also his reputation, his honor, his legacy that were being destroyed. It was not death alone that he was facing, but a shameful death, a fact that would have figured largely in a time when one's name was something to be guarded.

Even though it eventually came out that he was innocent of the crime with which he had been charged, apparently such vindication did little to ameliorate his spirit's bitterness. Soon after his death, strange things began to be reported in the house he had lived in. And these strange things persisted, and have continued to persist, for centuries, binding the old colonial building to its past. Today, the Michael Swope House on 210 Prince Street is known as one of those places in old Alexandria where history refuses to die. That isn't such an odd thing in Old Town Alexandria, where an abundance of colonial architecture ensures the city's history is not going anywhere. Neither, it seems, is John Dixon's ghost.

No one can say when exactly he made his first appearance, or how his spirit first manifested itself, but it would have been

*The Michael Swope House is known as one of those places in Old Alexandria where history refuses to die.*

sometime in the late 1700s, not long after he was executed. Since then, there have been ongoing accounts over more than two centuries.

The piano was one early sign of Dixon's spirited presence. Early residents spoke about how the instrument would come to life in the middle of the night. More than one dinner party was interrupted by the strains of some Mozart sonata as invisible fingers danced over keys with surprising skill. Although witnesses were almost always more troubled than impressed by this display, Dixon's ghost had it in him to be more unpleasant.

There were times when certain rooms in the Michael Swope House suddenly became very cold. The cold was occasionally known to get so intense that people were able to see their breath in the middle of an otherwise sultry summer night. And though dramatic cold spots definitely have a way of making people feel unwelcome, Dixon's ghost did not need to go so far as to fiddle with the temperature to make people feel uncomfortable. Sometimes, simply being present was enough.

Throughout the years, more than one person complained of feeling an intangible "presence" or "force" that did not want them there. Not so much a physical cold, it has been described as a cold nonetheless, a feeling as though one is coming under the gaze of a disapproving eye, though there is actually no one there. More than once, this immaterial other has driven people away.

One of the better-known instances occurred in the 1930s when the house was up for sale. According to the legend, the house came to the attention of a woman from England who expressed interest in buying it. Her tour of inspection started well. She was taken through the layout of the ground floor, and there was no sense of creeping hostility as she was guided through the second floor. The dark confines of the root cellar, the supernatural ground zero of any stereotypical haunted house, checked out fine. But when this woman got on the staircase to go up to the third story, she was instantly overwhelmed by a vague, yet all-too-real, sense that she was not welcome.

"This house is not mine." The words came, almost unbidden, from her lips. "There is someone here who does not wish to be disturbed." Not knowing anything of the house's haunted past, she said that there was some sort of force on the stairway that was barring her way. It was literally impossible for her to continue any farther.

Concluding her visit without seeing the third floor, the woman later claimed that she would have been very interested in buying the house but knew in her heart that it would not please the presence residing there. She knew it beyond any doubt, claiming that she was, and always had been, sensitive to the presence of ghosts. Her words have been quoted by L.B. Taylor in his seminal work, *The Ghosts of Virginia*: "I'm very psychic, and I can tell you that there is definitely a ghost in this house—one that, for one reason or another, does not like me." While Dixon's ghost was capable of exhibiting distaste for guests, he was rarely this inhospitable. What was it specifically about this woman that aroused such ire?

Well, she was British. It has been proposed that her accent may well have triggered a negative memory for him who had been executed by those who spoke with similar inflection. It seemed that, after two centuries, the spirit of John Dixon still harbored a hatred for the British.

For the most part, though, Dixon's ghost seems content to share his living space. Cold spots and ominous impressions aside, he still enjoys playing the piano and has been known to actually appear on the staircase from time to time, a hazy apparition dressed in knee-length pants and long stockings.

Perhaps in time his anger will fade and he may move on to whatever netherworld is beyond his house. Or maybe Dixon's ghost has gotten comfortable at the Michael Swope House and is entirely prepared to spend another two centuries there. Whatever the case, it is still advisable that any visitors with British accents keep their voices down. The American Revolution was a long time ago, but if anything can be said about the 210 Prince Street haunting, it is that the ghost of John Dixon knows how to hold a grudge.

# The Ghost of Crazy Bet

Richmond, Virginia, 1864. A lone woman makes her way down Grace Street. "My, the lilacs are fine this time of year," she says, stopping in the middle of the street to look at an iron lamppost with appreciation, as though it were covered with flowering blossoms. She stands there for a while, long enough so that a passing group of women sees her. "I say, aren't they something?" she says to them, pointing at the lamppost. "They are the most beautiful lilacs I think I've ever seen."

"Sure, sure," one of the women says wearily. "They're beautiful, Elizabeth."

"Poor girl," another one adds as they walk by. "See what happens when a lady fills her mind with all that Northern nonsense. Girl forgot her roots. To think she came from one of our best families. Now look at her."

"Shoo, Crazy Bet!" yet another says, giving her a gentle nudge in the rear. "Get yourself to wherever you're going. This isn't any way for a lady to behave!"

And so Crazy Bet continued on her way, babbling incoherently to herself, wild eyes darting up and down the desolate street. Some of Richmond's citizens had gotten used to the sight of her marching back and forth between her family's grand home on Grace Street and Libby Prison, where Union prisoners of war were being held. For others, the sight of Crazy Bet never got old. She was a living morality tale, staring wide eyed from under a tangle of loosely tied hair, in a once-grand ballroom dress now filthy, patched and threadbare, carrying a worn basket under her arm. It was a common refrain among the society women of Richmond: "Elizabeth Van Lew.

She came from one of our best families, but then her father, poor man, got the notion of sending her up to Philadelphia for her schooling. She came back with all sorts of *ideas*. Free the slaves and preserve the Union and all of that. Poor girl forgot where she was from. Look at her now."

There was some truth to the story. Elizabeth had indeed come from one of Richmond's wealthier families. She was the favorite child of John Van Lew, a wealthy antebellum Virginian who only wanted what every other Southern patrician wanted for his daughter—marriage to a wealthy and honorable suitor. Elizabeth, however, had other ideas.

Rebellious from an early age, Elizabeth Van Lew had disagreed with her father for most of her life. She had no interest in attracting a man or getting married. And how could she worry about such a thing as marriage when their home was staffed entirely by slaves? Yes. Young Elizabeth was not only imbued with a generally disagreeable disposition, she was also a budding abolitionist. Nevertheless, John Van Lew delighted in his spirited daughter, convinced that she would calm down when she got older.

To this end, he sent her off to Philadelphia to be educated, which, if he had given it more thought, was probably not the wisest thing to do if he was trying to get her to conform to Southern mores. In the mid-1800s Philadelphia was the largest city in the United States, a teeming industrial center that represented everything the traditionally agrarian South was not. What was more, it was one of the centers of the Northern anti-slavery movement.

When she returned to Richmond, Elizabeth was determined to spread the word of the immorality of slavery, taking every opportunity to pontificate. It didn't matter where she was or whether her audience was willing to listen. Her father could only watch as Elizabeth turned every party he threw into a political meeting by voicing her extreme, and very unpopular, views with the zeal of the most dedicated Northern abolitionist.

In the years leading up to the Civil War, Elizabeth not only thwarted her father's best efforts to introduce her to eligible suitors, but also managed to cast the Van Lew family name into disrepute among the Richmond elite. They retaliated against Elizabeth's politics with laughter, dubbing her "Crazy Bet" and turning her speeches into a running joke. As for John Van Lew, in a time when honor and reputation were the pillars of a man's status, his daughter's scandalous behavior was a liability he did not outlive. Given what Elizabeth became during the Civil War, it is probably a good thing that he passed away before the war's opening shots were fired at Fort Sumter.

*       *       *

Crazy Bet approached Libby Prison. Her dress was stained with mud from when she tripped over her hem and fell. A group of soldiers had been standing nearby when it happened and had laughed raucously as she pulled herself to her feet, flailing her arms and hollering at the ground as though the mischievous earth had attempted to topple her. "Easy now, Bet!" one of the soldiers had hollered. "Keep it up and you're gonna hurt the dirt's feelings." She had echoed the ensuing laughter with maniacal gusto and then continued on her way to the prison.

The Confederate guard at the gate smiled kindly as she approached. "Miss Van Lew," he said with a nod.

*Elizabeth Van Lew's mansion*

Suddenly, the mad spark in her eyes faded. She looked the soldier straight in the face and smiled back at him. "Good afternoon to you, Private," Crazy Bet said. "How are you doin' this fine day?" Reaching into her basket as she walked by, she pulled out a flask and handed it to the young man. "Something to help you bide the hours."

He took the flask with an appreciative smile and stepped aside. "The Yanks will be glad to see you, I reckon."

"God's charity takes no sides in this terrible war," she replied. Elizabeth was already past him, walking into the prison compound. She stepped with a purpose she did not have outside the gates. Her face was suddenly serious, and she was silent, no longer endlessly spouting nonsense as she had been on the streets. Once inside, she headed straight for the prisoners, greeting every Confederate soldier she met with a friendly smile, dispensing little homemade gifts here and there.

She was in a room with two Union soldiers now, a private and a lieutenant. She was administering to the private, changing the bloodied bandage wrapped around his forehead, while speaking to the lieutenant. "I brought you boys a bit of home cookin,'" she said, gesturing to her basket. "I know how terrible the food can be in this place."

"Thank you, ma'am," the lieutenant said, reaching into her basket and finding a freshly baked pie. "Much appreciated."

"No need. Never let it be said that Elizabeth Van Lew isn't a gracious hostess to folks visiting Richmond," she said, smiling.

The lieutenant smiled back, but something in his face changed when she mentioned her name. There was a seriousness that wasn't there before. "Well, Miss Van Lew, I've heard a lot about Southern hospitality, and I'm glad to see that this war hasn't killed it." Yet, as the lieutenant spoke, he pulled a small piece of paper from inside his jacket and slipped it into Elizabeth's basket. The private didn't notice. Neither did the Confederate guard who had just walked by. But Elizabeth did, and she gave him a small nod.

She didn't waste too much time after that. When she finished bandaging up the private, she put her medical kit into her basket and grabbed the piece of paper. In a single, quick motion, she buried it in the big, unruly bun atop her head. "God look over you, Lieutenant," she said, and she left.

On her way out, the guards did a quick search, looking through her basket to make sure she wasn't smuggling anything out. The search was halfhearted. While Richmond's society women didn't think much of her, the Confederate soldiers stationed at Libby welcomed her daily visits. As far as the guards were concerned, Elizabeth Van Lew was above suspicion.

Back outside, Elizabeth Van Lew was Crazy Bet again, hollering at walls, flailing her arms and tripping over her dress. Passersby hollered insults, laughed condescendingly or cast piteous looks. No one paused to consider that she had been at Libby Prison practically every day since the war broke out.

At first, no one paid attention to her visits. Almost everyone in Richmond knew about Elizabeth's political beliefs at the outset of the war, and, initially, her behavior raised many eyebrows. Almost every day she administered to Union soldiers who had been captured. But when a group of Richmond women invited her to help make a battle flag for one of the local regiments, she declined. The war suddenly became very real when the casualty lists started coming in. That was when certain people began to pay close attention to what Elizabeth was doing, and her daily trips to Libby Prison came under suspicion.

Then she lost her mind—she began appearing on Grace Street with uncombed hair and in a filthy dress, shouting at the air. To those people who had thought her activities suspicious, all it took was the sight of Crazy Bet stumbling toward Libby Prison, the object of so much ridicule and pity, and those suspicions were lifted.

The instant Elizabeth was back inside her house, she regained her composure. Making her way straight to her study, she called one of her father's former slaves. Her first action after her father had passed was to free all the family slaves. Nevertheless, some had stayed on of their own free will. Now a number of them aided her in her operations.

She pulled the lieutenant's note out of her hair and looked it over quickly. It was a list of active Confederate units the captured Union officer had observed from behind enemy lines. Wasting no time, she told her collaborator that the information must get to the bluecoats as quickly as possible. The woman who ran the message across to Union command was as good at her work as Elizabeth Van Lew, and the next morning General Ulysses S. Grant had the lieutenant's observations on his desk, along with a small bouquet of flowers.

Elizabeth kept up this operation through the course of the war: playing crazy for her daily walks to Libby Prison; intelligence-gathering visits with Union prisoners; sending what information she had gathered across the front line to Union headquarters. By the end of the war, these reports had become so regular—and so reliable—that General Grant had come to expect them every day first thing in the morning.

Elizabeth would pay a heavy price for her role. She must have been eager to shed her Crazy Bet façade, which she kept up for so many years. The first thing she did when Grant marched into Richmond in April 1865 was hoist the stars and stripes up the flagpole over her house. The sight of the enemy's flag flying on Grace Street attracted an angry mob. Richmond residents had endured too much heartache over the course of the war, and they were getting angrier by the minute. The mob grew in size as shouted insults turned to threats.

When the front door opened, the woman who was standing there bore no resemblance to the crazy woman they had come to know. Elizabeth's hair was combed, her face was scrubbed, and she was wearing a brilliant dress. She stood and stared at the gathered throng.

"Crazy Bet, you old spinster!" someone shouted. "You best take down that Yankee rag, or someone might do somethin' you might regret!"

There was a sudden hush as Elizabeth Van Lew stepped forward and pointed a stern finger at the man who had shouted at her. "I know you, sir; I know where your family lives." Her eyes turned to another one of the faces—one of the women who had mocked her mercilessly for the last five years. "I know you as well." She looked at the woman for a long moment before pointing to yet another among the crowd. "You as well. In fact, I don't think there are any strange faces here. Well, neighbors and friends, surely you know that General Grant will be here in about an hour's time. That's something y'all should think about before you go ahead and do something rash." The silence that fell over the crowd was part shock, part fear, and Elizabeth let it hang there for a moment or two before finishing. "If anyone does a single thing to my home, or anyone inside, I promise you that person's own house will be burned to the ground before noon."

No one felt compelled to test whether or not she had these kinds of connections with the occupying army. They dispersed, realizing then that all that time they had had a spy in their midst—that Crazy Bet wasn't crazy at all but just putting on an act to distract them from her tireless subterfuge.

*Crazy Bet could be seen walking to the Libby Prison every day.*

General Grant himself would publicly acknowledge Elizabeth's contribution to the Union war effort, and rewarded her with an appointment as Postmaster of Richmond when he became president. Still, despite the victory of her anti-slavery convictions, and such open praise by a president, Elizabeth spent the rest of her life paying for her role as a Union collaborator. And paying dearly.

After its military defeat, the South was made to endure a famously difficult Reconstruction. No one in Virginia had anything good to say about the Northern order that descended upon them, an order to which Elizabeth herself was inextricably linked. Never did a society produce a greater pariah than Richmond did of Elizabeth Van Lew.

She was a strident abolitionist before the war and her unpopular views had won her nothing but mockery and scorn. But when her role as a Union spy became known, the popular reaction went far beyond hatred; she was marked an outcast for the rest of her life. It was as though Richmond's population all at once decided that she no longer existed. Ignored by all, she was completely excluded from every social event, and no one responded to invitations she sent out. There were no longer sneers and catcalls when she walked down the street. She wasn't Crazy Bet anymore, but a traitor, and, in those first years following the war, no one so much as looked at her. She became invisible, a living ghost. People loathed, shunned and eventually forgot her.

It was a harsh sentence, and it left Elizabeth a profoundly miserable woman. Enduring such scorn, she survived the rest of the 19th century a shadow of her former self. The prolonged isolation robbed her of the considerable intelligence and energy she once possessed. When she wasn't cooped up in her grand home on Grace Street, she could be seen walking aimlessly through her neighborhood. She hobbled by her fellow townsfolk without even glancing at them, babbling, instead, to herself—or else shouting at the walls and lampposts—just as she had years ago, on her way to Libby Prison, when she was only pretending to be crazy. It was this constant muttering that brought her old alias back to life, as new generations of Virginians took to calling her Crazy Bet. This time, the sobriquet was all too fitting.

Elizabeth Van Lew died in 1900, an 82-year-old woman who fulfilled her life's goal in her 40s; then spent the rest of her years paying for it. She was laid to rest in Richmond's Shockoe Cemetery, but her story does not end there.

The sightings began shortly after her death, when residents living on Grace Street spied the emaciated figure of old Crazy Bet hobbling down the same road she did when she was alive. She was seen only in the evening, making her maniacal way to some unknown destination. Many people turned and ran from the shambling apparition, horrified at the sight of Crazy Bet returned from the dead. Yet those who overcame their fear and endeavored to take a closer look were always disappointed. After walking no more than three blocks, Crazy Bet just vanished into the air.

Elizabeth's apparition continued to be reported until 1911, the year her home was demolished. After that, her supernatural jaunts ceased. Although there have been sightings in the area of a strange-looking woman wearing a hopelessly anachronistic dress since then, they have been so far and few between that it would be a stretch to say Elizabeth's ghost still haunts Grace Street. Yet it could be entirely possible that Crazy Bet's spirit occasionally returns to the city that despised her so, if only to visit the site of her family home. Perhaps she admires Richmond's lights sprawling above Grace Street while reflecting on her part in the eradication of slavery in the United States.

# The Ghosts of Nelson House

There is a certain colonial quaintness to it—the cannonball still embedded after more than 200 years in the brick gable of Yorktown's most famous building. Any local history buff is able to tell the story, which has taken on the stature of national myth. It was during the War of Independence, when the ardently patriotic governor of Virginia, Thomas Nelson, Jr., was so resolved in his opposition to the British Empire that he turned his cannon against his own hometown.

On October 19, 1781, American patriots laid siege to General Charles Cornwallis' fortified position in Yorktown. Nelson, Jr., was the commander of the Virginia militia, and even though the British were on the verge of being expelled from the colonies once and for all, his feelings about the whole affair must have surely been divided. On one hand, Nelson was as firm a patriot as a man could be. He had been present in Philadelphia in 1776, where he put his signature on the historic Declaration of Independence. He had been appointed a major general in the Revolutionary Army, and had wholeheartedly committed his family fortune to the cause.

But here he was, looking over Yorktown, the town of his provenance, where his father had made the family fortune. Through his telescope, he could see the three-story home his father had constructed—the same home that he was born in. He was attached to this home the way lords must have been to their estates. After all, the Nelsons were almost considered nobility here in Virginia, and their house was the colonial equivalent of a castle. But now it was General Cornwallis' headquarters, and British and Loyalist forces now occupied Yorktown—his enemies. Here, Thomas Nelson, Jr., experienced firsthand that particular horror of civil war, where the enemy so often ends up being a man's neighbors, friends, family. And the battles often ravage places that the combatants love.

So it was with Major General Nelson on this late October day, the cannon of his militia loaded and leveled at his hometown, waiting only for his command to open fire. He could see the house his father had built, the streets and alleys he ran through as a child. Glancing at the rows of artillery arrayed next to him, he saw the town's ruin. And he gave the order nonetheless.

The bombardment began in the next roaring instant, as cannonballs rained down on the streets of Yorktown. It was said that Nelson expressly ordered his commanding officers not to spare Nelson House from the artillery barrage. That Cornwallis had made it his headquarters made it one of their targets. The evidence of Nelson's determination is still there: the famous cannonball fired during the famous barrage, lodged between two attic windows—a symbol of one man's uncompromising determination and the fierce emotions woken during the conflict.

And yet this occasion wouldn't be the only time Nelson House was situated in the midst of American bloodshed. Flash forward some 80 years into the future, when York County would once more become the focus of violence, this time in a far more brutal clash.

The Civil War was raging across the country, and General George McClellan was marching for Richmond, pushing the Army of the Potomac up the Virginia Peninsula toward the

Confederate capital. He was stopped in York County when advance scouts reported General John Magruder's small force of Confederates entrenched in and around Yorktown. The order of battle was common enough by Civil War standards in that the Confederate forces were severely outnumbered: Magruder's 13,000 fighting men versus McClellan's near 90,000. Also, like so many military battles of the Civil War, the onset of the Yorktown engagement saw the Union brass being out-maneuvered by the Confederates. Although there were nearly seven bluecoats for every graycoat, Magruder had deployed his men so that McClellan believed himself to be facing a larger force.

Yet Magruder's ruse did not keep McClellan at bay indefinitely, and it was not long before the casualties began to stream in. The Confederates used Nelson House as a field hospital during the ensuing siege of Yorktown, and the historic colonial estate with the Revolutionary War cannonball protruding from its surface was transformed into a grisly site of agony and horror.

Medical practices during the Civil War were brutal. The surgeons, largely overworked, unqualified and uninformed medical professionals, worked in extreme septic conditions so bad that almost every soldier put under their knives was practically guaranteed to develop a major infection. The doctors did not have the time or the skill for thorough examinations, and most of them treated wounded extremities by hacking them off. Thus field hospitals were terrible places, identifiable after major engagements by the bleeding piles of arms and legs stacked around them. It was commonly acknowledged that the surgeon's operating table could be more dangerous than the battlefield.

Magruder's stand at Yorktown was really only a holding action; the outnumbered Confederate force retreated in
late April 1862, just before McClellan was about to begin his
attack in earnest. The real battles of what would eventually
be called the Peninsular Campaign took place farther north
along the neck of land bounded by the York and James riv-
ers. It was only when McClellan's massive force approached
Virginia's capital that the Confederates launched a series of
bloody engagements from May through to July, eventually
driving the Union advance back.

The fighting at Yorktown was light compared to the violence that would follow. Although casualties were relatively
small—the Confederates lost roughly 140 men—there were
still more than enough dying and wounded to fill the rooms
and halls of Nelson House.

To deal with the sudden influx of wounded soldiers,
a basic triage was set up where incoming casualties were
placed on designated floors according to the severity of their
wounds. Men with minor wounds were treated on the first
floor, those who needed amputations were mostly on the second, and those mortally wounded, considered beyond medical aid, were put in the attic, where they were left to die.

It was hell. Overcrowded with irreparably mangled bodies,
the attic was becoming saturated with blood. As the Union
soldiers advanced, everyone in town could hear the moans,
shouts and screams of the doomed souls—the mortal regrets,
the fervent prayers, the shouts for loved ones. Most of us have
never come face to face with our mortality, and so it is difficult to imagine how a soldier gasping his last breaths might
act. While one man might give in to fear, another might pon-
der the meaning of his sacrifice, utter final prayers and find

*During the Civil War, medical professionals, often overworked and unqualified, treated soldiers' wounded extremities by simply amputating them.*

the determination to die with honor, or submit to despair. None of us knows what all those men whose final moments were spent in the Nelson House attic were thinking as they succumbed to their wounds.

The hell in the attic did not remain for long. Nelson House was emptied when the Confederates vacated Yorktown, after which the old colonial burg was under control of Union forces for the remainder of the war. Strategically relevant during the early phases of McClellan's Peninsula Campaign, it gradually receded into the national memory as the war ripped through the rest of the country. Nevertheless, if the Civil War never visited Yorktown after that, it had been there long enough to leave its mark. Nelson House would never be the same.

Very few people talked about it in the following decades. True, there had been stories of strange goings-on inside the house before the onset of the Civil War. There was one story, often brought up at tea parties and in schoolyards, about the spirit of a British soldier that was in the house, still seeking cover from the artillery barrage that had claimed him so long ago during the Revolutionary conflict. It was said that his favorite hiding place was under a secret staircase located behind the dining room wall. But there were times when he emerged, sending cutlery, dishware and ornaments sailing through the air as his fearful moans drifted through the house.

Although the account of the British soldier had circulated for some time, few took it seriously; even fewer approached it with any trepidation. The legend of the purported haunting gathered a nostalgic tinge, a harmlessness. This anonymous soldier was a reminder of a colonial time long rendered romantic. If anyone were actually to catch sight of the ghostly redcoat, the expected reaction would be more one of wonder or glee rather than fear. Given the terrible conditions in the attic during the Civil War, however, far more frightening phenomena were said to be going on in Nelson House after that war was over.

Until 1907, when the Nelson family finally sold the old house, very few people were able to confirm any of the rumors circulating about the building. Only the Nelsons and their servants could say, and they were very guarded about what—if anything—they saw within the four walls of the family home. During this time, what information there was came mostly from visitors, who told of sudden drafts that blew through hallways and rooms and that were so cold that they crept into the bones, eliciting violent shudders in the height of summer. Those who inquired about the source of these drafts were treated to stuttering explanations of open windows, or else strained silence. Other guests emerged from the house with stories of heavy shadows moving quickly in the corners of their vision, flitting shapes, black and humanoid, that would dissolve into nothingness the instant startled visitors turned to look at them. Not that a person had to be invited to the Nelson House to get a sense that things there weren't quite right. On some nights, passersby were filled with an inexplicable sense of foreboding after a mere glance at the attic windows from the street.

After the Nelsons moved out, the historic house became widely recognized as haunted. It was the angry spirits, people said, of those mortally wounded Confederate soldiers who died in the attic in April of 1862. Between 1907 and 1968, a succession of owners all spoke of the ghostly residents that

*Spirit activity is prevalent on the attic floor of Nelson House (on the right).*

lived at Nelson House with them. They talked about the severe chills that descended suddenly, making hairs stand up on necks and arms, the agonized moans in the middle of the night, the heavy footsteps echoing through the hallways.

And always there was the attic. Residents quickly learned to avoid the top floor, which was dark and musty on the best of days. That is, the days that it wasn't thick with the smell of dry, stale blood that was intense enough to send bystanders running for the stairs, gagging as they went. While some people who ventured up to the attic left with a vague taste of mortality, others came face to face with the dead—a black figure, standing in the corner of the attic. Described as the looming shadow of a man, without a man casting it, the figure had been known to chase horrified visitors from its haunting space.

Today, Nelson House, along with the accidental memorial embedded in the wall, has become a popular destination for history buffs. Like all things colonial, the house is imbued with a definite cultural cachet. Purchased by the National Park Service in 1968, Nelson House was fully restored and made into one of the central attractions in Yorktown's Colonial National Historical Park. People have come from near and far to visit the town where the War of Independence was effectively over, and the Peninsular Campaign of 1862 met its first resistance.

Yet many visitors to Nelson House who go hoping to experience a piece of America's colonial past often walk away with something else altogether—bizarre and unsettling experiences that have kept the legend of Nelson House alive. Over the years, numerous patrons have heard the pained moans from the top floor. More than one individual passing by at night has looked up at the attic windows, suddenly overcome with the sense that something was staring back at them from the darkness within. Far more disturbing encounters have been reported. In her book *The Hauntings of Williamsburg, Yorktown and Jamestown,* Jackie Eileen Behrend writes about a woman named Cindy Murphy. She and four friends looked on in terror as the attic window slowly slid open and the face of a heavily bleeding man emerged from within, glaring fiercely at them. Having heard the stories of the Nelson

House ghosts, Murphy knew with a single glance at the face above that she was looking at a dead man.

Who knows how long these spirits will remain there, stuck in their final moments of fear and agony? Perhaps their passing was so traumatic that they will remain there as long as Nelson House's mortar holds. Or maybe someone just needs to tell them that the war is over. They've done their duty. They can now rest.

# The Phantom Soldiers
# of Petersburg

By March 1865, even the most zealous Confederates were finding it difficult to deny the now-inevitable end of the Civil War. The Shenandoah Valley was controlled by Union forces, the strategically essential port of Wilmington, North Carolina, had fallen into Northern hands and there was not a single regiment in the Confederate Army whose uniforms were not bullet ridden or blood stained. The Southern states had put up a hell of a fight, but after roughly four years of war, they found themselves outnumbered, out-supplied, out-maneuvered and on the brink of total collapse.

And yet the will to fight still burned in Robert E. Lee. Union forces were converging on Richmond; Sherman occupied Atlanta; New Orleans had been overrun by blue-coats; and Lee's famed Army of Northern Virginia had been holed up in Petersburg for over nine months, besieged by the numerically superior Army of the Potomac. But Lee was unable to concede defeat, even as his demoralized men were deserting by the thousands.

First, he needed to get his army out of Petersburg. The vaunted fighting force was able to do little while contained there, effectively trapped within the intricate web of trenches the Union army dug around the town. Lee's strategy for victory had always been centered on battlefield victories, but he needed to get his army back on the move to score more victories against Grant's Army of the Potomac. Even though his men were hopelessly outnumbered, and few among them had the nerve or energy for another prolonged campaign,

Lee looked to continue the struggle. He gave General Gordon the order: "Find a gap in their line that we can slip our army through. We must break out of this trap within the month, or all is lost."

After three weeks of gathering intelligence, Gordon returned to Lee with his report. They had indeed found a weakness in the lines—Fort Stedman. Located near the Appomattox, on the Union's right, it stood a mere 150 yards from Confederate trenches. It was close enough to come under a sudden attack. The plan was to launch a surprise raid under cover of darkness and capture the fort, thus securing the breach in the Union line. The logic was that such an attack would put pressure on Grant to call in soldiers from his extended lines, thereby allowing for a general attack on the diverted Union forces and a potential breakout. General Lee was under no illusions. It was a reckless attack—a frantic, near-hopeless attempt to keep the struggle for secession alive.

Even Lee, however, might have been surprised at how well the first stage of the attack went. Ironically, the crumbling morale of the Confederates was largely responsible. Over the months, Southern soldiers had been deserting in droves, so that the guards at the Union pickets had become used to seeing Southern soldiers crossing the battlefield under cover of darkness. Sentries did not feel there was much cause for alarm, then, when the first group of Confederates emerged from their trenches at four o'clock on the morning of March 25. Further, these men were actually posing as deserters—armed deserters, that is, thanks to a Union mandate that allowed enemy soldiers to surrender their arms for $10 a rifle. The attack on Fort Stedman began quietly, in the dark hours before sunrise, and was won without a shot being fired. The rag-tag first wave, hungry, lean, unkempt, and utterly convincing as deserters, cowed the Union sentries into surrender by the tips of their bayonets. The assault on Fort Stedman itself followed, and the garrison there, caught completely by surprise, capitulated almost immediately.

The reserve units moved in fast, rushing through the breach to take the three artillery batteries that supported the fort. Victory again was theirs, as the soldiers manning the cannon were quickly overrun. Here the battle reached its critical juncture, where the momentum of the Confederate attack might carry the day if the Union command did not react. Luckily for the bluecoats, Brigadier General John Hartranft was a capable and decisive commander. He gave the order, and Union regiments were quickly brought to bear on the breakthrough. They came even as the Confederates began to flounder. Gordon's ordered offensive balked and then stalled. It was the dark. They could not find their objectives and were having difficulty making their way through the enemy trenches in the early morning. Hartranft's men began their counterattack in earnest.

As the entire Union line woke to the sound of gunfire, General Gordon would have known that the breakthrough attempt was all but lost. Nevertheless, he would not give up Stedman without a fight. His subordinates could hear the desperation behind the order to hold the fort. And, remarkably, for a few hours they did, despite the ever-increasing intensity of the Union counterattack. It was a brief, bloody fight in which the Confederates fell steadily before the swelling numbers of Union solders. By 8:15 that morning, the word came down the line: Fort Stedman had been retaken by the bluecoats—roughly four hours after the attack had begun.

That four hours cost about 1000 Union men and anywhere from 2700 to 4000 Confederates. The morale of the hungry attackers was low, and many of their losses were certainly desertions—losses that General Lee, still somehow scheming up possible victories, could scarcely afford. Meanwhile, the relentless Grant sensed the failed offensive had further weakened Lee's position and pressed his advantage, ordering a series of attacks along the Southern line and drawing ever closer to Petersburg.

Thus the attack on Fort Stedman was thwarted, a minor assault that in the end achieved nothing. The inauspicious raid was one of General Robert E. Lee's last operations. On April 9, just over two weeks later, Lee finally laid down his colors, surrendering the Army of Northern Virginia in the town of Appomattox, ushering in the end of the Confederacy and the American Civil War.

According to some, the conflict never truly ended for those men who fought around Fort Stedman in the dying days of the Civil War. Indeed, given the sights and sounds that are reported around the old battlefield to this very day, there are more than a few Union soldiers who have lingered on the old battlefield long after the call of duty expired.

The site of the bloody siege was designated the Petersburg National Battlefield on August 24, 1962. Although it is difficult to know what sort of stories circulated about the place before then, ever since a regular staff was hired to work in the park, the ghosts of Fort Stedman have taken a place in the canon of Virginia folklore.

Over the years, some park employees have been woken early in the morning, around six o'clock, to the noise of drums and bugles. A battlefield rally sounds crisp and close, as if a Civil War regiment was organizing itself just outside. Those who have gone to investigate the source of the din are always confronted by the same eerie stillness when they open their doors. A moment ago the morning was a cacophony of drum roll and bugle call; now only the trill of a bird or the leaves whispering on a mild breeze punctuated the silence.

This phenomenon isn't the only one said to occur near the Petersburg battlefield. Early morning visitors are the ones who have the best chance of witnessing the row of phantom soldiers. They are seen arrayed near the fort, along a ridge where a contingent of General Hartranft's men assembled before launching their counterattack against the Confederates. How many ghostly bluecoats appear vary depending on who is telling the story. Some claim to have seen a handful of them, while other shocked witnesses have said the ridge was covered with deathly silent men in Union gear standing at statue-like attention, their faces expressionless.

In utter silence they remain, staring with leaden gazes right through those witnessing their lack of activity. No one has thought to time how long the images last. Some people state that it cannot be for over two or three minutes; others speak of it feeling like an eternity. And then the soldiers just vanish—abruptly, without warning—leaving eyewitnesses struggling with a strange sense of sadness. This sadness has been described as a sudden and overwhelming awareness of these men's sacrifice, men who died mere weeks before the war came to an end.

# The Loudoun County Dead

Everything seemed to change the day the grotesque flotilla of dead Union soldiers arrived in Washington, D.C., borne through the country's capital on the gentle waters of the Potomac. There were dozens of them, floating down river in terrifying repose, their blue uniforms creased and soaking, lifeless grimaces on their bone-white faces. They were only a few dozen killed in a war that ultimately claimed hundreds of thousands, but the news of their approach sent a spasm of fear through Washington. It was late October 1861. The Civil War had just begun, and the public was still adjusting to the idea of casualties. Few people in Washington were ready to deal with the consequences of war, let alone stare the dead in the face as they floated by. Those bodies not intercepted by fishermen eventually washed ashore on the streets of the nation's capital; except, that is, for a single bloated corpse that floated straight through Washington, continuing downstream before being deposited in front of Mount Vernon, the historic home of George Washington. There could hardly have been a darker or more fitting omen for the coming horror of the Civil War.

The dead soldiers were casualties from the battle at Ball's Bluff, a small but disastrous Union offensive on the town of Leesburg, 30 miles or so up the Potomac from Washington. From the beginning it was unclear what the Union command hoped to accomplish by the assault. History tells us that the commanding officer of the Army of the Potomac, General McClellan, was uneasy about the Confederate presence in Leesburg, Virginia, and sent orders out to General Charles

Stone to make a "slight demonstration" that might "have the effect of moving the Confederates" from their position. What this "slight demonstration" was, exactly, was left to the imagination of General Stone, and so the Union general ordered his ill-fated amphibious assault across the Potomac River.

The attack commenced early in the morning of October 21, with Colonel Edward Baker leading a group of soldiers across the Potomac River under cover of darkness. Colonel Baker was one of the Union army's celebrity officers. Although he had almost no military experience to speak of, he earned his rank from his distinguished civilian career. He had been an elected senator prior to the Civil War and was a personal friend of Abraham Lincoln's. On orders from General Stone, the celebrated—though untested—colonel led over 1000 men across the Potomac and up Ball's Bluff, a steep embankment looming over the Virginia side of the river.

Baker's landing on the southern bank was a rather chaotic affair, hamstrung by a shortage of boats and the hard ascent up Ball's Bluff. By the time the Union men were ready for the march on Leesburg, a Confederate force under the command of the battle-hardened Brigadier General Nathan Evans was ready to receive them. What followed was an unmitigated disaster for Baker and his men.

General Evans, veteran of the First Battle of Manassas, commanded a force essentially equal in size to that of Colonel Baker's. However, he enjoyed the advantages of defense and a skilled body of soldiers under his command—advantages that he brought to good use soon after Baker's men crested Ball's Bluff. Baker's men had barely begun their advance toward Leesburg when they met determined Confederate resistance. The fight was fully joined soon after midday, with sharp fire being exchanged up and down the Confederate and Union lines. Under pressure of the Confederate attack, the Union advance halted, wavered and then began to fall back. The turning point had come when a Confederate sharpshooter picked Colonel Baker off his horse early in the fighting, killing him in plain sight of most of his men. By six o'clock that evening, the Union soldiers had been pushed all the way back to the Potomac, their backs to the edge of Ball's Bluff's sheer drop on the verge of a panicked rout, barely able to hold their wavering line together.

Recognizing that his adversaries were near the breaking point, General Evans deemed it was time to deliver the coup de grâce, and ordered his men to charge. The shrill whoop of the rebel yell sounded over the battlefield, and, all at once, over 1000 Southern men rushed the Union soldiers teetering over the Potomac. Whatever resolve was left in the Northern ranks dissolved before the oncoming line of bayonets, and the thin blue line stretched along Ball's Bluff broke apart. The chaos of the last moments at Ball's Bluff was such that it resonated across the United States, a terrified tremor that spread from the shores of the Potomac to Washington, D.C., through the streets of New York and into the farthest flung Michigan backwoods.

Stuck between the oncoming Confederates and the steep drop into the Potomac, the Union soldiers had nowhere to go. Hundreds of them took the headlong plunge down Ball's Bluff, skidding and tumbling into the river, their enemies firing down at their backs as they ran. It was here that many of the Union dead were picked up by the Potomac's current and carried downstream to Washington. As for those men who made their stand on the top of the bluff, they found it

*Bodies of the slain in the Potomac, 1861, in a drawing by Alfred R. Waud*

in themselves to continue the fight for another hour or so before sudden and outright surrender. By eight o'clock that night, the Confederates were marching over 700 prisoners to Leesburg.

General Stone's defeat at Ball's Bluff enraged the Northern public. Although it was a relatively minor engagement compared to other Civil War battles, it had a major impact on popular perceptions of the war. Ball's Bluff followed close on the heels of the major Union defeat at the Battle of Bull Run.

It was a complete defeat at the hands of an equal foe, saw the loss of a prominent colonel and had its casualties float through the heart of the nation's capital. Someone had to take the fall for this terrible blunder.

The focus of the public's ire fell on General Charles Stone, the senior officer who ordered the advance over the Potomac. It didn't matter that the general wasn't on the battlefield and didn't give a single field command—the people needed a scapegoat, and Stone was offered up on the altar of public opinion. In the wake of the battle, Congress established the Congressional Joint Committee on the Conduct of War and promptly had General Stone arrested for what they called "the most atrocious blunder in history." Stone spent over five months in prison, set free only when the furor over Ball's Bluff died down.

Although Stone was given a military commission after he was released from prison, he was never able to rid himself of the stigma of his failure at Ball's Bluff. It haunted him to his grave. As it turned out, he wasn't the only one haunted by it. The Ball's Bluff National Cemetery was established shortly after the war, in December 1865. With a mere 54 Union casualties buried there, it was, and remains, the smallest military cemetery in the United States. But what it lacks in size it has certainly made up for in infamy.

Stories of strange activities in the cemetery and surrounding battlefield began circulating not long after the first visitors came and went. It is impossible to say who witnessed them first—the disembodied shouts in the darkness, the painful wails, the battle cries, the faintly shimmering apparitions running toward Ball's Bluff. Year after year, people continued to witness these phenomena. Of course, there was little question about the origin of these sights and sounds. People were quick to point out the misguided Union offensive and ultimately vain sacrifices of the dead soldiers buried in the cemetery. Could the spirits of these men be as angry about the loss at Ball's Bluff as the public was? Were their appearances at the National Cemetery an expression of the trauma of their last moments, their ire at having given up their lives for naught?

If so, there is reason to believe the spirits there are still fixated on their untimely deaths. Even to this day, almost 150 years after the battle, the ghosts of Ball's Bluff are said to still haunt the field where they fell. Over the years, the number of inexplicable encounters has made the Civil War battlefield into something of a supernatural landmark. The stories have been repeated so many times that most residents of Loudoun County living near Ball's Bluff barely give them a second thought. Or the adults don't, anyway. Among local teenagers, the Civil War ghosts continue to be something of an attraction.

Especially since the 1950s, Loudoun County kids have taken to driving out to the old battlefield at night, looking for thrills. These weekend excursions have usually been nothing more than excuses for them to party, and any Civil War ghosts hoping to be noticed would have to make a lot of noise over the rambunctious, often semi-inebriated, cavorting youths. Yet while these teenagers have been able to shout over the ghosts more often than not, enough nocturnal forays have ended in supernatural encounters that the legend of Ball's Bluff has been kept alive.

The ghosts usually make their entrance with a cacophony of screams, shouts and wails along with the rumble of gunfire and cannon. The sounds are distant at first, and then grow

clearer until the darkness is alive with the sounds of anachronistic battle, causing bushes to tremble and boughs to shake.
That is when a sudden chill descends over the area, and vague
outlines of soldiers are seen darting around the cemetery,
moving to the direction of unheard commands. We might
imagine the reaction of teenagers as the ghosts emerge from
the night, waging their supernatural battle all around them.
Some witnesses stay put far longer than others, but they inev-
itably all end up running for their cars, intent on getting out
of the area as fast as they can.

It is at this point that the spirits of Ball's Bluff demonstrate
the full extent of their power. Cars revved into a hasty retreat
have been held in place by some invisible and unyielding
force. Tires spin and engines whine, but the vehicles remain
stationary, straining against the inhuman strength, until they
are abruptly released after about half a minute, sent roaring
away from the cursed battlefield. Evidence of the encounter
is always the same, visible when the frightened teenagers feel
they are far enough away to stop their cars, step out and look
for any damage. They are there every time, year after year—
two enormous handprints of muddy clay slapped on the back
of each car.

The ghosts at Ball's Bluff have been expressing their aver-
sion to automobiles since the 1950s, and, given the stories
that continue to circulate, the dead soldiers share the same
dislike for 2003 Honda Civics as they did for 1957 Chevies.
We can only guess why the ghosts have remained behind and
why they continue to relive their battle before the terrified
eyes of curious teenagers. Maybe they have lost all concept of
the passage of time and keep fighting for Ball's Bluff because
they have never been able to get over the terror of their final

moments. Or perhaps they remain behind in their hope to impart some lesson of the futility of war. Whether their spirits are possessed by a mission or an unmitigated madness, their lingering presence has succeeded in keeping the country's smallest national cemetery on the map and ensuring that their sacrifice is not forgotten.

# The Man in Gray

It was during the dark years after the Civil War, in that famous time called Reconstruction, when Virginia, along with the rest of the South, was being forced to cope with the aftereffects of a devastating and ultimately futile struggle. Widespread misery at the massive human cost, economic depression, social upheaval—from South Carolina to Texas, Georgia to Arkansas, the scars of the Civil War ran deep.

In Virginia, the wounds of war were especially ugly. It had as much to do with geography as it did with politics. Virginia contained both the capital of the Confederate States and the Shenandoah River Valley, the lush "bread basket of the Confederacy." As such, it was a key supply region for the Southern forces and a major objective for the Union forces. It was also the northernmost Confederate state, the first and most important territory the Union forces had to march through on their way south. To say that Virginia was accessible to the Union army isn't putting it quite right. It was unavoidable. Any military strategist at the time would have called the impending violence inevitable. And so it was. The First and Second battles of Bull Run, Fredericksburg, Chancellorsville, the Peninsular Campaign—more blood was spilled in Virginia than in any other state.

And within the embattled Old Dominion there were few places more chaotic than its northwestern region, Appalachian territory, bordering on hostile West Virginia and the gateway to the vital Shenandoah Valley. The counties of the northwest were ravaged by the war. Attack and counter-attack raged across this area of the state. It has been said that the town of Winchester, in Frederick County, went back and forth between Union and Confederate possession between 60 and 70 times during the war.

Waverly Mansion, an old colonial house built more than a century before the onset of the Civil War, was situated about five miles from Winchester, right in the midst of the brutally fought-over territory between North and South. Local legend tells us that Waverly, too, was touched by the horrors of the war.

For the longest time, he was just "the Man in Gray." According to legend, one of his earliest appearances occurred sometime after the war's end, when Virginia was well into the gloom of Reconstruction. Lily Jolliffe, a Frederick County woman traveling to see her father, was spending the night in Waverly's guestroom over the ground-floor parlor. Bolting the door and blowing out the lantern, she had just begun to fall asleep when heavy footsteps broke the early evening calm. Assuming that it was Waverly's hostess approaching for a word before going to sleep, Lily sat up groggily, thinking to unbolt her door.

But she did not even make it out of bed. Before she was able to throw back the covers, the bolt slid back, the door flew open, and a towering silhouette of a man appeared in the doorway. She could only stare, agape, as the man strode into her room. Moving with urgency, he went straight past her bed without looking at her. He stopped in front of the windows, where he stayed for several seconds, carefully studying the view. Lily, holding her breath and blanket clutched close, almost screamed when the man turned his attention away from the window and moved, suddenly and quickly, to the foot of the bed. He stood and stared for several long moments. There was just enough light for Lily to make out basic features. His face was grizzled, and he was glaring at her with frightening intensity. She could see that he wore the gray uniform of a Confederate officer, but she was not able to make out his rank. The man stood glaring for several silent moments before abruptly turning and storming out of the room.

When Lily met her father the next day, the incident with the gray-clad officer was the first thing out of her mouth. If she was expecting shock or incredulity at the end of her story, she would have been disappointed. Her father had a story of his own.

A Civil War veteran himself, Lily's father had spent the days after Robert E. Lee's surrender at Appomattox in a sullen haze. Not sure whether to celebrate the end of the homicidal brutality or mourn the defeat the Confederacy, he and three other soldiers from his regiment rented a room at Waverly, where they promptly proceeded to gamble and get soused.

As it turned out, the room they rented was the same room that Lily herself was staying in—the guestroom over the ground-floor parlor. The four soldiers had candles on the tables for light. They were playing cards with what little they had and were well on their way to drinking the worst memories of the war temporarily from their minds. Forgetfulness would not come on this night, however. Partway through a hand, the guestroom door flew open and a man in a Confederate uniform treaded into the room. They could see by the candlelight that he was pale and grizzled and had a fierce glare. Though the war was over and the Southern army in ruins, the habit of military discipline almost brought the former fighting men to attention. The stranger was an officer, that was obvious, but before any of them were able to make out his rank, he swept an angry arm over the table, and all the candles went out. Gripped by a fear none of them could understand, the men bolted from their room. They stopped at the end of the hall, waiting for the stern officer to emerge from the darkened room.

Five minutes, 15 minutes, the better part of an hour—the intruder did not come out into the hall; there was not so much as a peep from within. After some time, the four men finally got their courage up. They walked toward the guest-room all together, shoulder to shoulder down the hall, so that no one would be in front of another. They reentered the room. Surprise? Fear? What word exists to describe what they felt when they relit the candles and discovered the room empty. The card table was exactly as they left it; the window was still shut and locked from the inside. There wasn't a trace of the terrifying officer that they all swore they had seen.

While Lily Joliffe and her father's accounts mark the earliest tales to emerge from Waverly, they would definitely not be the last. According to legend, a number of strange, inexplicable occurrences have been observed at the Frederick County mansion since the end of the Civil War—phenomena that go beyond the occasional appearance of an angry Confederate officer in the guestroom above the parlor.

The Man in Gray has not stopped appearing before frightened visitors. Unsettling as these sightings are, they are marked by a definite consistency. He always appears after dark, barging into the same room with the same urgency. He never lingers longer than a few minutes and usually does not leave without subjecting the witness to a hard, unflinching glare.

No one can say for certain what the Man in Gray is hoping to accomplish in the room above the parlor. Over the years, he has never attempted to communicate with those he has left so rattled by his random appearances.

Although it might seem that there is neither rhyme nor reason to the Man in Gray's appearances, the same cannot be said of one of the other happenings at Waverly.

Twice since the end of the Civil War, clocks in the mansion have reportedly acquired a disturbing prescience. The first incident occurred in the late 19th century when a woman named Dabney Harrison was living there. Mrs. Harrison claimed to have had numerous encounters with the Man in Gray, so many that she actually grew to accept sharing her home with the glowering apparition. The thing that happened with the clock in the hallway, however, was much harder for her to accept.

The clock had been broken for quite some time, so Mrs. Harrison was surprised, to say the least, when she was woken in the middle of the night by the chiming in the hallway. She immediately recognized the sound of the long-silent clock and was filled with a terrible sense of impending disaster—a dread that seemed disproportionate to what was actually happening. A broken clock chiming on its own would elicit some degree of curiosity or fear. But this paralyzing horror was in a woman who had learned to cope with the semi-regular appearances of an angry apparition. And yet all Mrs. Harrison could do was lie there—wide-eyed, heart pounding—counting every time the clock struck. By her count, it chimed exactly 79 times before falling silent again.

The very next day, a messenger came by Waverly to tell Mrs. Harrison that her grandfather had passed away the previous night. He was 79 years old.

About a century later, the latest residents at Waverly had a similar experience with their own hallway clock. This one had been a recent gift from a friend, brand new and in fine working order when they got it. Then, one night, shortly after they had placed the clock on the wall, it stopped running. The next morning, they got a call that the friend who had given them the clock had died in the night.

Local folklore enthusiasts have long been aware of Waverly's past. No one has been able to offer any explanation for the apparent power of the mansion's clocks, but the same cannot be said of the mysterious Man in Gray. In the October 1993 issue of the *Winchester Star*, a reporter named Linda McCarty unearthed a piece of the building's past that may shed some light on the origin of Waverly's infamous apparition.

In her article, McCarty identified a Confederate officer from North Carolina, a Colonel Charles Christopher Blacknall. He was a commander of the 23rd North Carolina and was badly wounded in the battle of Third Winchester. His foot shattered by a Union rifle ball, Colonel Blacknall was hastily treated in a field hospital and then sent to Waverly to recover. Given the notoriously septic conditions of Civil War medicine, a smooth convalescence was too much to ask. It was soon discovered that the wound had become infected, and, as gangrene began to set in, Colonel Blacknall's leg had to be amputated. The Confederate officer did not live for long after the traumatic procedure. The official cause of death was attributed to "intestinal and digestive problems" but would have assuredly been related to the infection and amputation.

The conclusion, of course, is that the Man in Gray is the ghost of the dead colonel, who was possessed of such a powerful will to fight that his spirit remained vigilant even after his body had quit. Yet, as vigilant as the colonel may have remained, there is only so much a disembodied spirit can contribute to a war. In Colonel Blacknall's case, this was not very much at all—limited to frightening former Confederate soldiers away from their drunken cavorting and then terrorizing the odd individual sleeping in the guestroom above the parlor.

Although it has taken many years, it seems as though the colonel has slowly grasped the futility of such gestures. While the sounds of disembodied footsteps and slamming doors have continued to be heard from the second floor hallway, it is said that there has been a marked decrease in such phenomena over the decades. Furthermore, there were no confirmed sightings of the Man in Gray throughout most of the 20th century. One can only conclude that the poor Confederate has finally decided to leave the Civil War behind him.

As for the strange power the clocks in Waverly have exhibited, residents may draw some consolation that they have warned of upcoming mortality only twice in the mansion's lengthy history.

# 3
# Modern Ghosts

# Josephine Doesn't Like Bluegrass

It had been in Josephine Corbin's family for over 80 years. At 913 North Main Street in Danville, it stands: the commanding two-story building built of brick and accented with impressive ironwork. Built in the 1880s, it was the only home that the reclusive Josephine had ever known. Her father had died within its walls in the late 19th century, shortly after it was built, and her mother passed on in the 1940s. Josephine alone remained there until her death well into the 1960s. She was a proud and solitary woman who, scarcely seen in the final two decades of her life, was something of a local mystery to the citizens of Danville.

After her mother died, she spent virtually all of her time shut up behind the imposing brick walls of her family home. And within those walls, it was said, she rarely ventured from her bedroom, a small, dimly lit chamber with a fireplace on the second floor at the back of the house.

People knew little about Josephine Corbin. It was said she had been a striking young woman with dark hair and brilliant blue eyes. But little else about her has survived. Without doubt, her name would have been easily forgotten were it was not for the fact that, for a short period in the 1980s, the doors to her family home were opened to the public. The former Corbin residence had been converted into a restaurant called the Victorian, and for a brief time became one of Danville's more popular eateries. The clank, clatter and bustle of a lively restaurant soon shattered the tomb-like silence that had long prevailed over the old home. The restaurant only lasted

*View of Danville*

for a handful of years, but, during that time, patrons of the
Victorian came to know the name of Josephine Corbin.

Without exception, all the bizarre phenomena that were
said to take place occurred in what used to be the back bedroom on the second floor—Josephine's bedroom. The owners
of the Victorian had converted that room into a separate dining room, which patrons who desired a little privacy could
reserve for a quiet evening, or a relatively quiet evening,
anyway. Compared to the stillness that surely hung over the

chamber when Josephine lived there, the noise generated by a table of diners would be the equivalent of a full marching band.

All things considered, the ghost of Josephine was quite good about the conversion of her house. Although it is not unknown for spirits, annoyed by the commotion of the living, to set upon their quarry with icy hands, eerie chills, physical disruptions, and all-around creepiness, Miss Corbin was not nearly so aggressive. Her manifestations were so innocuous, often just enough to suggest she was there, that some might think she enjoyed the company. Or perhaps she enjoyed it *some* of the time, when the company was not playing bluegrass.

Many people became aware of Josephine's presence by the sound of footsteps on the ceiling, an occurrence that would not have been such a big deal if there had, in fact, been a third floor above the room. It was not an uncommon thing for a table of diners to fall silent when those slow, measured footsteps began to make their way across the roof. "There goes Miss Corbin," new diners might have whispered in delight, while those who had experienced such a thing before might have tried hollering a greeting, which would always, unfailingly, go unanswered.

This is not to say Josephine Corbin never interacted with her busy new housemates. It was not unknown for waitresses venturing into the room after closing to be greeted by light peals of laughter. The waitresses' reactions would naturally depend on their respective dispositions. Some would run out of the building; others would stay on and calmly finish their shift, deciding that there was nothing sinister or threatening about the laughter.

The only time Josephine expressed anything that could be called displeasure was when she did not approve of the musical selection. As a rule, she did not like anything that was too energetic and exhibited a special dislike for the lively strains of bluegrass music. Without fail, whenever someone decided to play bluegrass, the speakers in the dining room would instantly go out, only coming back on when some gentler form of music was put in the stereo.

Some might be surprised to know that the presence of Josephine's ghost did not hurt business at the Victorian. Rather, the haunted dining room was always one of the busiest parts of the restaurant; there was never a shortage of people eager to have an experience with the former resident. The room became a local news item. As one Danville journalist wrote:

> *There is a haunting air of the past about the ornate red brick mansion that houses the Victorian. The atmosphere in the elegant restored house can be almost chilling, especially in the back dining room. For it is in that room that the willful ghost of Josephine Corbin is said to walk.*

As far as the local fame went, it helped that she was such a striking woman, and that her likeness was hung up on the dining room wall. Mounted in an oval frame, the portrait captured Josephine as a young woman, and while some people casually passed over the painting, many others found themselves captivated by it. There was something about the eyes, the way the vivid blue orbs seemed to glow with an eerie intelligence, an awareness. More than a few people believed that something of Josephine's essence was somehow contained in that disturbingly lifelike portrait—that she was in fact watching the guests through the bright blue pigments that depicted her eyes.

This portrait was not the only image of the ghostly resident. Photographs taken of the haunted room revealed a shadowy outline of a female figure standing by the fireplace. So it would seem that, after decades of solitude, Josephine found herself entertaining guests, and not just a few of them—she had more visitors set foot in 913 North Main Street than when she was alive. It is impossible to say how she felt about this fact, but, given how calm her manifestations were, she could not have been too bothered by it. And if she was, at least it did not last for long. After the Victorian closed down, a married couple purchased the building and turned it back into a private residence.

If Josephine Corbin's spirit was stirred by the influx of so many strangers, how did it react to the sudden decrease in activity? Well, she did nothing to make the new residents too uncomfortable. And although there was some evidence of her continued presence, she seemed to become less active as the number of people in her former home lessened.

The footsteps on the ceiling have ceased, as has her need to impose her musical taste, but she has persisted in other ways. On one occasion, the owner claimed to hear a strange drumming noise when he stepped into the back bedroom. The drumming stopped when he walked out, only to resume when he reentered.

This man's wife had experienced strange phenomena herself. Sometimes it was nothing more than a feeling, an inexplicable yet undeniable sense that there was someone else in the room with her. Then there were instances when she swore she felt something brush by her in the back bedroom, as though an unseen individual was squeezing past her.

As one might expect, the number of accounts involving such ghostly encounters have decreased dramatically since the house became a private residence. Whereas the varied stories coming from the mouths of the Victorian's patrons once kept the legend alive, now there is little being said. Still, we might expect Josephine Corbin to linger on in her little room at the back of the house, much quieter than she was before, since there are far fewer guests to entertain.

# The Banging in the Night

He lives just outside of Richmond, in Powhatan County. He's a retired man who chooses just to go by the name "Joe" while talking about the goings on in his country home—bizarre events that, for a while, had him wondering about his sanity. "I've never been a superstitious kind of person," he begins, "talking about spirits in the hills, or Tommyknockers, or whatever else old folks used to tell their kids to keep them out of the woods at night. Always figured it was a load of nonsense, until I got old myself. Now here *I* am doing the telling."

Joe laughs as he voices the following caveat: "Who knows? Maybe you do have to be old and half-crazy to see ghosts. Hell, cheese goes bad after a while—brain gets mushy, too, sitting up there for so long." This light-hearted retiree says that there were many mornings, when, waking up and remembering what had transpired the night before, he wondered whether his own gray matter was curdling or if he was just having incredibly vivid dreams.

"The thing about it is that I spent quite a few years there before and never had to deal with any sort of nonsense. I'd go out every odd weekend and on holidays to get some quiet away from the city. Kept it up for quite some time, y'see, and nothing weird ever went on." Joe had no reservations, then, about spending more time out at his country home after he retired. Preferring city life, his wife was never too enthused about the place, but Joe always knew that he would make it a second home after he retired.

"It didn't bother me, really, going out there by myself. Gave me a chance to do a lot of reading, recharge my batteries. Bet if you asked the missus back then," he adds with a chuckle, "she'd tell you that she didn't mind me going out too much, either. Then again, I never had it in me to tell her about what started happening out there. She probably would've had me committed, or else made me go talk to a priest." Neither option struck Joe as pleasant, and not wishing to worry anyone about things he might or might not be witnessing, he decided to keep the events to himself. "I've only told two of my closest friends about it," he says, "and, as far as I know, they're the only people who know."

Until now.

When he was still working, Joe said he would usually make it out to the country once or twice every month, usually for no more than two days each trip. Things changed dramatically after he retired. With all sorts of time on his hands, he began spending more time away from his house in Richmond.

"Sometimes, I'd spend as much as one week out there at a time. On them longer stays, I'd usually have one or two pals along with me, but a lot of the time I was out there by myself. Just the quiet, the trees and a few good books."

He was enjoying his time in his second home well enough, even though he was on his own more often than not. "I took to it just fine. Kept busy during the days, and at night, well, I never was one with a wild imagination. I didn't ever get the heebie-jeebies out there. Didn't even cross my mind that anything was wrong."

Then, one summer night, everything changed. "I remember it real clear-like," Joe says, recalling the sound that woke him from his slumber. "First thing I did was look at my clock. It was just past three in the morning, and I was lying there wide awake, wondering what the hell was going on." Never a fitful sleeper, Joe was not used to waking up in the middle of the night for no good reason.

"It took me a few seconds to figure out that my heart was pounding away like a jackhammer," he continues. "It was a strange feeling—like I was scared, but God knew of what. I looked around my room, but it was me and me alone in there." Still, this was little assurance to Joe, who, in his state, could not help but notice menace in every darkened shape and shadow. The window on the wall opposite him was especially unsettling. It was open; the curtains were back, and there was something about how the tree branches and bushes were swaying that made a chill crawl up his back.

"I think I remember sayin' to myself that I must've woke up from one hell of a nightmare. That would've been fine, though, if the hairs on my neck weren't standing straight up and my heart wasn't beating like it was in a parade. It was like this. Either something wasn't right, or I was going right out of my mind."

What happened next hardly cleared things up for him.

"I was like that for probably two or three minutes, even though it felt like way longer, and I was just thinking about getting up and turning the lights on when it all started."

Joe says he was so startled that he shouted when the silence was broken by three loud bangs on the wall next to the window. "I was wound up pretty tight, I've got to say, and when I first heard those bangs, I pretty well jumped clean out of my skin. There was a second, I think, when my heart thought about blowing up on me." Yet, as hard as the shock may have been on his ticker, it did jar him into action.

"It was all action stations after that," Joe says. "I grabbed my back-scratcher like it was a baseball bat and went straight for the window, shouting at whoever was out there that he better get the hell out, 'cause I meant business." Joe was at the window seconds later, but there was no visible culprit, just the bushes and the trees and the still sounds of the night.

"My thinking at the time was that it was some fool kids messing around, having fun with the old guy, but no doubt I was still right spooked. Fool kids these days are a bit different than the fool kids we were when we were growing up," he says. "Seems to me these days they don't know when they've crossed the line."

Joe laughs a little at this summation, and then pauses. It's a loaded silence. "Thing about it is," he finally resumes, "looking back, if I'm honest about it, I was way more rattled than I should've been if it was just kids. That didn't explain why I woke up feeling like the Devil himself was out there looking back at me. When I was standing there looking outside with that damn back-scratcher in my hand, I think there was this voice in my head that was telling me something weird was going on. It probably had something to do with how quiet it was out there. Kids would've been laughing or whooping or shoutin.' I'd hear 'em running at least, and there was no sound of a car on the road."

Nevertheless, Joe admits that he felt much better telling himself that it was nothing more than basic mischief—something he could act on. Joe continues: "I went out to the porch right quick, trading my back-scratcher in for my shotgun on my way out. I won't lie about it," he says. "I flicked the light on, stood out there on the porch with my gun and told whoever was listening that I wasn't going to put up with any garbage."

Joe would discover soon enough that his mysterious visitors—or visitor—would not be so easily deterred. "It took me a while to get to sleep after that," he says. "I locked that window and drew the curtains, kept my gun close and was listening real close." But nothing came, and Joe's vigilance gradually gave in to sleep. "Next morning, I woke up and was thinking: *What a downright messed-up dream.* But then I saw the shotgun by the bed and the curtains drawn, and I changed my mind."

Not entirely. Unable to completely accept the bizarre events from the night before, Joe decided that it very well *could* have been a dream that he walked through. Either way, whatever unease had descended the night before dissolved before the morning sun, and he found it easy enough to push the events to the back of his mind. For the rest of that weekend there were no repeat occurrences, and Joe went back to Richmond thinking that his experience that one night was less than he had made it out to be—young pranksters, perhaps, that had gotten to him more than they should have.

"I was okay with letting the whole thing go," Joe says. "Kept it to myself and pretty well forgot about it." He goes on to say that as the days went on, the notion that the whole thing actually was a dream seemed ever more likely. "All it took was a bit of time. Two or three weeks later, when I was driving back out for the weekend, I don't think I was even thinking about it."

He may have forgotten all about it, but Joe would soon discover that things were just getting started. "I remember the second time around real clearly," he says. It was his first night back at the cabin, and he woke up overcome with the same sense of heart-pounding dread he felt the first time. "It was 3:17, exactly, and just like the first time, I felt like my heart was about to break out of my ribs." Having experienced this once before, Joe reacted much quicker. "I was out of my bed in a shot, and even though my legs were shaking like crazy, I grabbed my gun out of my closet and went straight for the window."

The banging began when he was halfway across the room—four heavy knocks that made the windowpane vibrate and sent a spasm of fear through him. Joe says that he did not slow down, though, and had just started shouting a challenge when he reached the window. "I was near as angry as I was scared, and I don't think the words that made it out of my mouth are fit to print," he says. "But I didn't get much out, anyway, 'cause when I got to the window, there was nobody there."

It was shock that silenced him then—shock and incomprehension. "Thing about it was that whoever it was banging on my wall, there was no way in the world he could've been pounding away like that and then make it away without me catchin' sight of him. Just impossible—plain and simple."

Explaining that there weren't three seconds between the time he heard the pounding and when he arrived at the window, Joe attempts to explain the unexplainable. "The bush was about 10 to 15 yards away from the house, and if a guy wanted to vanish quick, that's pretty well where he'd go," he states. "But that night, it was right impossible for someone to move that fast. No way. Even if there was someone in the bush anyway, there were no sounds coming from there. They weren't movin' a speck either."

Ignoring the unease creeping up his back, Joe went out to investigate, a flashlight in one hand, his shotgun in the other. "I took a look around but didn't see a thing," he says. "Not a trace of the son of a gun. Not even any footprints around the window where I heard the banging." Joe spent the next little bit doing his rounds outside, being as thorough as he could be while also working out the inexplicable terror that had numbed him in his bedroom, admitting that it felt good being up on his feet and looking around. There was comfort in action; he was not just lying there being toyed with. This series of events was a mystery, and he was doing what he could to solve it.

Much of Joe's subsequent investigations may be attributed to the comfort aspect of activity. If he wasn't getting answers, looking for them helped ameliorate the extreme, almost paralyzing terror that came with the late-night banging. It was good that he had discovered this coping strategy, given the frequency with which the events began to occur. "Things got sort of blurry after that," Joe says. "I remember that time out, I heard the banging one more time, the last night I was out." He recalls running outside that night as well, only to find himself alone in the darkness again, not a trace of whoever or—as Joe was increasingly beginning to suspect—whatever was responsible for the banging.

It continued regularly from then on. If Joe would go out to his country home for three nights, he could expect to be woken in the middle of the night at least once—his heart pounding in his chest, that icy fear crawling up his back. The banging near the window would always follow, but no matter what measures he took, Joe found it impossible to catch his persistent visitor in the act. Not that he ever gave up.

If anything, Joe just became more determined to get to the bottom of the banging. He acknowledges it became something of an obsession. Never once after that first time did he shut the window, draw the curtain or hope that the thing outside would leave him alone. No. Joe needed to know what was going on. "I'll admit," he says, "I got a bit strange about it for a good while."

Strange?

By strange, Joe means that he began investing in home-improvement and surveillance equipment. "First thing I did was hook up a floodlight with a motion detector," he says. "This thing was so bright that when it came on, I could see about three or four yards into the trees." Bright as it was, it did little good when whoever was banging seemed to be able to do so without triggering the motion detector.

"I do remember that night I had the light put in," he recalls. "Man, I must've fallen asleep that night with a smile on my face, thinking for sure I got that sucker now." Perhaps when he was woken by that now-familiar spasm of fear, he had that same smile on his face, too. "The light was still off when I got up, and I remember thinking that maybe there wasn't going to be a knock this time, and it could have been that I woke up out of habit, because whatever was doing the knocking couldn't be there. It didn't trigger the light."

Yet the inexplicable cold persisted, and, in another moment, Joe's rationalization was about to be completely confounded. He was just about to close his eyes when, suddenly, four heavy raps sounded against the wall. "That time, I remember that the window actually shook. That's how loud the banging was." Yet the motion-detector light had not come on. Rushing to the window, he was greeted with the same darkness, and not even a hint of movement in the bush. "That time hurt pretty bad," Joe says. And yet as discouraging as the incident was, it did nothing to kill his determination. He went outside again to see if the light was working. When it switched on the second he rounded the corner, he was able to draw a conclusion: nothing could have gotten close enough to the wall to bang on it without triggering the floodlight. He was now certain of one thing, at least—whatever was knocking on the exterior of his house was not, could not be, a solid, material figure. It could not be human. "Crazy as it was, I'd been thinking along those lines for a while; now I knew for sure."

Joe had managed to go his entire life without giving ghosts or the afterlife too much consideration; now he found himself trying to track one down outside his country home. How did he feel about this? "It's something I've been living with for a while," he says, "so it's tricky to say exactly what was going through my head when I knew for sure that I was dealing with something—that was not of this world."

Anyone with a trace of imagination might have at least entertained the possibility. Waking up suddenly in the middle of the night with a pounding heart and goose-bumps just in time to hear four loud bangs against the wall, it isn't hard to see how speculation might lead a person to make unconventional conclusions. Joe was a self-professed "rational man" who had avoided the snares of superstition for most of his life. Now, for the first time, he was ready to admit that he was confronting an entity that, to use his words, "was not of this world."

"I guess for a while there, I wasn't ready to accept that there was a ghost creepin' around my house," he says. "But you'd be surprised. When I opened my mind to it, like, when it hit me that there was no way in hell that I was dealing with anything else, it turned into a simple fact—same as the sun comin' up in the morning and going down at night. But I know full well what most people say about people who go around saying they got problems with ghosts. Do I believe in ghosts after seeing what I've seen? Sure I do."

Pragmatic as his attitude may have been, Joe went about pursuing the alleged ghost outside his house with a fervor— or, as he likes to say, he "got strange about it." The coming months saw him becoming more elaborate with his ghost-hunting attempts. "More than anything, I wanted to see it. You know…what was I dealing with here? Growing up, I heard a lot about the ghosts of old Indian spirits in the countryside. I also remember a few stories about the spirits of soldiers from the Civil War. There were some headless horsemen. The Bloody Mary. It's a hell of a thing when you start thinking that there might be some truth to those stories you always thought were nonsense."

Joe had decided that his visitor was indeed a supernatural entity, but what, exactly, did a supernatural entity look like? Was it an angry old Indian brave with feathers in his hair? A pale Confederate officer in a shimmering gray uniform? A livid witch hunched in the trees? If it was a matter of ghosts, of childhood legends, Joe was intent on seeing it for himself, no matter how elusive the thing was.

"Well, like I said before, it got sort of out of hand," Joe says. "I rigged the place right up. I had tape recorders all over the place—one on the windowsill, one on the ground right below the window, four others in the bush around that wall. Later on, I set up three video cameras on tripods—two of them against the wall by the window, and the other in the bush facing the siding of the wall." And Joe says that he always, *always*, slept with the window open and the curtains pulled back. Just in case he saw something himself, he kept his camera on his night table. It is safe to say there wasn't a better covered window in Powhatan County, if not the whole state of Virginia. Yet even then, the thing outside managed to evade him.

"The short of it is that I had all kinds of problems," Joe says. "The tape recorders were a real hassle. Every night I had them running, I had to set my alarm for quarter to three, go outside and turn them all on. Half the time, nothing would happen. As for the other half, when I went to check them after the banging, their batteries were usually kaput—dead, even though they were brand new." Joe says "usually." What did he get on tape those few times one or more of his recorders kept running?

Just enough.

"In the period of about six or seven months, it only happened a handful of times when one or two recorders were still going afterward. Each time, I got the exact same thing. You'd be hearing normal nighttime sounds; then, out of nowhere, right when they should've been recording the banging, there'd be this static noise, like the sound your TV makes when there's no signal. It'd last for about five, six seconds, then go back to normal."

These audio anomalies proved to be just enough to keep Joe going. Although he might have given up if his recorders continued to yield no results, the inexplicable static was proof that his tapes were able to capture something. He purchased the three video cameras with high hopes of capturing visual evidence of his otherworldly visitor.

"Those cameras told me about as much as those tape recordings did," Joe says. "Just like with the tapes, they had a way of going out on me, dying on full batteries, or else going all haywire when they should've been recording the banging sound." The fact that they would break out into static on those occasions when the batteries remained charged suggested to him that something was going on, even if he wasn't getting any hard evidence of what that something was.

"There was just one time with those cameras when I caught something that got me thinking, but even then, I can't say for sure if what I got was worth anythin' or not," Joe says. It was a fairly typical night in the way that he was woken shortly after three, just in time to hear the banging on his wall. After his obligatory look out the window for any sign of movement, he went outside to check his video cameras.

"Two of them were dead—surprise, surprise—but the third camera was still recording." Joe goes on to say that this third camera had been placed in the bushes, facing the window at an angle. It was a perfect vantage point. If there was anything to see, surely this camera had captured it.

"Breakthrough, right? That's what I thought," says Joe, who, eager to view the footage, watched the playback on the camera's monitor as he went inside. "There was no break in the recording, but I couldn't make out much on the display. You could see the window shaking a bit with the knocking, but that was pretty well it."

Pretty well it as it appeared on the camera monitor, anyway. After playing the sequence back several times, Joe was able to detect something, a small blur of light that seemed to be moving across the screen seconds after the knocks shook the window. It wasn't much, but it was enough to get him to plug his camera into the television set for a closer look. To this day, Joe remains ambiguous about the thing he saw.

"I've talked to people who do this sort of thing—take pictures of ghosts, get them on video tape," Joe says. "And going by what I've heard, maybe I got a bona fide ghost on tape." Yet he doesn't sound too sure—or impressed, for that matter.

"I gotta say, if I knew that was what I was waitin' for all that time, then I wouldn't have bothered." On his television, Joe could see it clearer, a vaguely circular blur of light moving across the screen right after the last bang on the window. "The sound died when it happened, so you can't hear the banging. But you can see the window rattle a little bit, and then the circle goes off screen. Orbs, they call them [the circles], but I was hoping for something a little more, I don't know, ghost-like. A man or woman or who-knows-what that you can see through. A glowing fog. I don't know—something besides a movin' speck of dust there one second and gone the next."

But for all his time and effort, this was the only solid evidence he would emerge with. "I gave up on the whole thing pretty quick after that," admits Joe. "Got tired of the whole thing pretty quick after that." He took a little break from the visits to his country home, opting instead to spend more weekends in Richmond. As for the waking nights and the mysterious knocking, on those weekends that he did go to his country home, he just learned to cope with them. He stopped bothering with his recording apparatus and stopped getting out of bed when the now-familiar fear gripped him in the middle of the night. Joe puts it this way: "It was easy. When getting spooked becomes routine, it's not nearly so spooky, you know what I'm sayin'?"

Today, the banging has stopped. And it has been silent for a while. Joe never heard it again after his wife passed. He has a theory that she took it on herself to shoo them all away on her way to the pearly gates. "It's made things a lot more quiet out there," he says. "And I appreciate being able to sleep through the night."

# Not Ready to Leave

When pressed to come up with a rational explanation for supernatural manifestations, many paranormal enthusiasts will offer a theory that bears some resemblance to a fundamental scientific principle, the first law of thermodynamics. This law states that energy that resides in a system cannot be created or destroyed but will often change, converting from one form to another. That is the way heat or thermal energy, when applied to a full kettle, will turn water into steam. Or how pistons in car engines convert combustion energy into mechanical energy. The parallel pseudo-scientific theory for ghosts begins with the assumption that people, like all other matter, are essentially made up of energy, and that this energy is *not*—indeed, *cannot be*, according to the first law—simply snuffed out when an individual passes away.

What happens, then, to this mysterious "energy"? The world's most established religions offer various answers as a keystone of their respective faiths. Certainly, those who feel more comfortable referring to this energy as the spirit, or soul, will likely offer one of these explanations.

Others will speak of the "psychic energies" existing all around us, on a plane we are, usually, unable to perceive. But every now and then, in places we call haunted, the psychic energies lurking beneath the world of perception rear up and become apparent in some way. These haunted places, so the theory goes, are sites where some traumatic, often fatal, event took place, leaving behind a "psychic imprint" or ghost that onlookers perceive reliving the trauma again and again for years, decades, even centuries. Anne Boleyn in the Tower of London, Julia Schuster in New Mexico's La Posada Hotel, the scores of uniformed dead said to haunt Gettysburg—the manifold traumas of earthly existence lie at the root of many famous ghost stories…and many more not so famous ones.

The following Norfolk resident expressed concern at the possible unwanted attention her story might attract. She requested anonymity and shall be called "Sara" in this account. "I've been living in this house with my husband and kids for a couple of years now," Sara begins, "but it's been in my family for way longer than that. My brother and his wife bought it about 16 years ago, then rented it out to my mom and dad when my brother got work out of state. After my dad died, my mom moved out, and we moved in."

Sara describes the residence as "a spacious old home" and goes on to say how attached her family has become to the place. "Thanksgiving and Christmas are always held here, and my brother's family always visits for at least a week every year. We've had so many great times here. Even with everything that's happened, I'd be surprised if my brother even thought about selling. It's the family house," she says, "and sometimes you've got to take the good with the bad."

That's Sara's attitude. Her mother, on the other hand, hasn't been nearly so compromising. Not that anyone can blame her. Just over three years ago, she watched helplessly as her husband suffered a fatal heart attack, drawing his last breaths while sitting in front of the six o'clock evening news.

"I got why she wanted to get out of there—or I thought I did," Sara says. "After going through what she did, I wouldn't feel too great about living there alone either. She started talking about moving out pretty quick after we buried Dad, but no one was rushing it too much." That was before Sara's mother took her aside and told her about what she'd been going through.

"I remember that afternoon like it was yesterday," Sara says. "For a month and a bit after Dad passed, there'd always been someone staying with Mom at the house. We made sure she was never alone." Until then, her mother had never expressed any desire to leave the house, but Sara knew from the moment she arrived that there was something very wrong. "She didn't look good at all. It looked like she hadn't slept in days, and she'd been crying just before I got there."

Sara instantly assumed that her mother was having difficulties with her grief and so was rendered speechless when her mother sat her down in silence, served a cup of tea and said: "Your father's still here. He hasn't left this house."

Sara's reaction: "Right away, I was really worried about her. What she was saying was so crazy, but she looked so serious about it. She was talking as though she were letting me in on some secret. Then she looked at the chair where he'd been sitting when he died and nodded at it." With that nod, Sara's concern was immediately tinged with apprehension—a whiff of fear that caused the hair on the back of her neck to stand on end. "Impossible as it was, there was a second when I was *sure* that he was there and she was looking at him."

The feeling was so strong that for a moment she doubted her better judgment and actually looked over her shoulder at her father's chair. No one was sitting there, but Sara admits that the sight of it made her uneasy.

"It also struck me that my mom needed more time," Sara says. "It'd been a month and all, but I felt just terrible about leaving her there alone. She wasn't ready to be by herself yet, that was all." Sara had no way of knowing how ready she really was because, right there, her mother started to insist that she needed to move.

"She wasn't taking no for an answer," Sara continues. "I told her that I'd sleep over there again, move in with her for a while, but that wasn't what she was after—at all. She was repeating herself, going on about how she had to get out of there, and started to get angry when I tried telling her that she needed more time."

Sara takes a moment to make something clear. "I should say that this was a pretty hard thing for me to take. This wasn't my mom at all. Between my mom and dad, all my life, my mom had been the steady one. I guess she was always sort of the strong, silent one. Whenever a problem came up—like trouble with the bills or my brother did badly on a report card—it was my dad who would get stressed and start worrying. My mom was the one who'd calm him down. You know, she always had a way of easing everyone's mind. Nothing seemed to get to her. So this thing she was pulling now was really getting to me."

Sara also admits that as she sat there next to her openly terrified mother, she began developing her own fear of her father's favorite chair. "You know, it was the way my mom kept looking at it. I could tell she was trying her hardest not to, but her eyes kept going that way. How she got so tense whenever she did, I started to get right squirrely about being there."

Deciding it was best for her mother that she did not push the issue—and possessed by a growing desire to get out of the house herself—Sara agreed that it would be best for her mother to stay with her and her family for a while. "Would you believe it?" Sara says. "She was already packed up and ready to go."

Three weeks later, Sara's mother was still visiting and showing no signs of wanting to go back home. "When I finally got the courage up to talk to her about it," Sara says, "she was definitely more like her old self about the whole thing."

Sara's mom was still adamantly against moving back into the house in which her husband died. She was able to calmly suggest, however, that if her presence was making things a bit too tight at Sara's place, then Sara's family was more than welcome to move into the empty Norfolk house.

When she realized that her mother was quite serious about the proposal, Sara decided that it was not such a bad idea. After all, she had always loved the place, and it was slightly bigger than the home her family was currently occupying. They could make good use of the extra space. Besides, it was perfectly understandable, wasn't it, a person's inability to live in the place where she saw her husband die? I went through this phase where I felt so guilty. I could not believe that we were so casual about my mom not moving back in there. We didn't even ask her. We even left my dad's favorite chair right where was when he died. It hit me that we'd been so completely thoughtless about it. I felt terrible." Sara's brother approved the arrangement, and they ended up switching houses just like that, roughly one month after Sara's mother had moved in with them.

By the time they'd relocated into the family home, the memory of her father's armchair had faded in Sara's mind. "You know, we've got boxes everywhere and the kids are running around and my husband's trying to figure out where he packed his ties," she says. "I pretty well stopped thinking about why we were moving there in the first place—because my mom couldn't be in the same room as my dad's old chair."

In the turmoil of the move, her father's armchair was largely forgotten, left in the living room as a serviceable piece of furniture. Evidently a pragmatic family, no one thought about linking the armchair to what had happened a couple of months ago. Then, four days after they had settled in, Sara's daughter appeared at her bedside in the middle of the night.

"That wasn't anything out of the ordinary," Sara says. "She's a sleepwalker and used to climb into bed with us all the time." Sara barely looked up but moved over to make room for her daughter. That was when her daughter spoke, and Sara realized that she was actually awake. "She shook me and said, 'Mom, Grandpa's downstairs.'" The words were whispered, but Sara was shocked awake. Her experience with her mother came back all at once. "I couldn't have seen myself getting out of bed if the situation was any different," she says, "but when I heard my daughter saying those words, I thought right away of what my mom told me that afternoon."

Instead of dismissing her daughter's story as the product of a child's dreamy imagination, Sara quietly got out of bed and took her daughter back to her bedroom. "My husband was the only person who knew the real reason Mom wanted to move out. He'd felt bad for her but didn't put anything behind what she saw, saying she was still coming to terms with my dad's passing. I was thinking then, or more like hoping, that he'd said something about it. I knew my mom wouldn't."

Sara asked her daughter what she had seen. "The girl was wide awake. She told me she'd gone downstairs to get some milk and saw that the TV was on. She went into the living room to take a look and saw her grandpa sitting in his chair, watching TV." Sara says that there was a queer seriousness to her daughter as she whispered what she had seen. "She was still too young to understand what death was about," she says, "and I think she was more curious than scared."

Sara asked her next question: "Did Daddy say anything to you about Grandma seeing Grandpa when we moved?" The silence that followed must have felt like an eternity, and when the answer came, it was with the same chill Sara had felt the day her mother moved out. "A mother knows her children," she says. "She looked at me and shrugged the way she'd look and shrug whenever she had no idea what someone was talking about." With that, it was obvious to Sara that neither her husband nor her mother had said a word.

"I tucked her in and told her that her grandpa was gone, that she must have been sleepwalking again, and that sometimes people think they're awake when really they're dreaming." Turning on the light, then, she read to her daughter until she fell asleep. After that, it was time to investigate.

"If you were to have asked me before, I'm not sure what I'd tell you about ghosts—whether or not they exist," says Sara. "One thing I can say for sure, though, is I've always been the kind of person who scared easy. I see a horror movie, and I'm thinking about it for weeks. My husband would laugh at me, but sometimes, in our old place, I'd feel a bit weird about going down into the basement when it was nighttime."

Still, Sara had made up her mind to go downstairs and see if there really was any truth to what her mother and now her daughter had told her. "I had this real bad feeling as I was going down those stairs," she says. "I didn't *want* to do it, but, for whatever reason, I couldn't see myself waking up my husband to take a look. Well, seriously, imagine it: 'Honey, can you go downstairs and check out the living room? Our girl just told me she saw a ghost down there.'"

About two footsteps from the bottom of the stairs was the open doorway that lead to the hallway off the living room—and what Sara saw when she stepped through that doorway made her stop.

"The TV was definitely on. I could see the blue light coming from the living room doorway, and I could hear some late-night television show. I'm not sure what was louder, though, the TV or my heart pounding away on me. Some people might say they'd be happy as anything to get the chance to see a father or mother that they'd lost, especially if, like me, they didn't get a proper chance to say 'bye' and all. Sure, sounds good, but let me say, standing there in that hall with the TV light flickering away, the thought of my dad being in that room scared me silly."

Sara pauses to qualify her fear. "I'd love to have the chance to talk to my dad, and if I believed for a second that my dad was actually in the living room, I'd be there in a shot. But if it really was my dad in the living room with the TV on, well, then it couldn't actually be my dad, but something that *looked* like him. Because if it really *was* my dad, there's no way in the world that he'd come back from the dead just to sit there in front of the television set. He'd talk to us. He'd want to know how we were doing. He'd do whatever he could to make us feel at home, not scare the living begeezus out of us."

Sara crept down the hall and, with no small degree of trepidation, peeked through the doorway into the living room. "The television set was on, but there was no one sitting in the armchair." Only after she switched the light on did she breathe easier. She turned off the television, deciding as she left that the armchair was going to be moved.

"The next morning, my daughter didn't say a word. It was like it never happened." Sara started thinking up explanations. After all, it was possible that her daughter had been sleepwalking again and turned on the television herself while she was unconscious. Maybe the television had woken her from a dream in which her grandfather had been sitting in the same armchair she had seen him in countless times. The entire episode could have easily gotten confused in her young mind. "The more I thought about it, the more likely it seemed my girl tried to tell me that she *dreamt* she saw her grandpa." In the light of day, the episode did not seem so sinister, and moving the armchair suddenly seemed to be more of a hassle than it was worth. So Sara was able to erase the episode as the vision of a sleepwalking dreamer.

Several days passed without incident, and Sara was just starting to watch television again without being aware of the armchair. Then, one night after an outing she came home to a sight that changed everything.

"I'd been out with a group of friends, and it was late when I got home," she says. "Everyone should have been asleep." Yet, from the foyer of her house, she could see that the television was on in the living room. "Well, I guess I had had a bit to drink and wasn't even thinking about what happened with my daughter." Assuming that someone was having difficulty getting to sleep, Sara casually strode down the hall and walked into the living room. "It's been over two years now," she says," and I still don't know how to describe how it felt to see my dad sitting there. It was just like my daughter and mom said. He was sitting in his favorite chair watching the TV. He looked real enough for me to touch."

Sara stresses that as much as the apparition looked like her father, she was looking at nothing more than a shadow of who her father had been. "He looked real, but it was obvious that my dad wasn't sitting there—a shadow is the best word I can come up with. It was just a shadow of my dad. None of my dad's personality was there, none of his life or intelligence." The apparition did not acknowledge Sara's presence in any way but sat in silence, staring expressionlessly at the flickering television screen in the corner of the room.

"Who knows how long I stood there?" Sara says. "It couldn't have been more than five minutes, but, looking back, I really can't say for sure." When Sara finally worked up the nerve to speak, it was a simple greeting. "All I could get out of my mouth was 'hello,' nothing else." When she spoke again, she managed to address him as her father.

"When I said, 'Hello, Dad,' he moved. He turned his head real slow until he was facing me. The way he was looking at me, he may as well have been watching the TV. A few seconds later he disappeared just like that."

Running upstairs, Sara wasted no time waking up her husband and telling him what had happened. "Poor guy," Sara laughs, "woken up by his half-drunk wife going on about how she just saw her deceased father in the living room. Now he says he was willing to believe what I was saying, but I'm pretty sure it wasn't until he saw for himself that he accepted what we were dealing with."

This acceptance would happen soon enough. "First thing we did the next day was move that armchair into the basement," says Sara. "I was thinking that there was nothing good about my dad, or more like a *piece* of my dad, showing up like that. It was hard enough for me to get my head around it; I can only imagine how hard it would be for my kids. Besides, back then I didn't think I was acting against my dad directly. Like I said, I just couldn't believe that there was anything of my dad in what I saw, and it really bothered me to see him like that—like some kind of weird, unreal version of what he really was."

Saying that she was planning on either selling or throwing out the chair the first chance she got, Sara settled with putting it in storage. "Everyone who saw him saw him in that chair," she says. "So put the chair away, and that's where the problem goes, right?"

She would discover soon enough that it would not be so easy.

"It happened the very next night, the same day we put the chair away," says Sara. "My husband woke me up that night. I remember his arm shaking my shoulder like mad, and the first thing that struck me was how cold it was. I'm talking *freezing*." Sara rolled over to see her husband sitting up in the dark, staring wide-eyed at the foot of the bed. Following his gaze, she sat up like a shot, looking on with the same wide-eyed expression. There, standing at the foot of the bed, was her father.

"My husband was having a hard enough time trying to breathe," says Sara. "So I did the talking. I asked him why he was in our room, and if he was the one that made it so cold. He had that same glassed-over look, so I didn't think he would say anything." She was right. Instead of speaking, the apparition turned his head to the television set in their room. The moment his gaze fell on it, the TV sprang to life.

"I'm telling you, right way, as soon as that TV went on, the cold was gone. We were back to room temperature just like that. He turned back from the TV, stared back at us for a few more seconds and then vanished like he did the night before."

The next day, Sara's husband was adamant that they get rid of the chair as soon as possible. Sara, however, was no longer so certain that that was the right thing to do. "I was getting the feeling that taking the chair out of the living room made him angry. My husband wanted me to call my mom and ask her about what she went through, but I didn't feel right about that. She'd already been through enough."

In the end, Sara agreed to her husband's demands. Not only did they move the chair out into the garage, with plans to take it out to the dump first chance they got, they also moved the television in the living room to their home office. Sara's husband also closed and locked the living room's sliding double doors. The rationale was that he was appearing in the living room but wouldn't be able to make his way around the house if they locked the doors.

As it turned out, a locked door did not prevent an angry apparition from venting its frustration. "I'll tell you, I had trouble sleeping that night," Sara says. "I could feel it in my gut that we'd done something wrong, that we weren't going to get anywhere by going against it. I was sure that things were going to get worse because of it." And she was right.

The first words out of Sara's mouth that night when she was woken by the sound of loud banging were, "Here we go." Loud thumps and crashes were coming from the ground floor as though things were being thrown, like heavy furniture was being overturned. "We were both up like a shot and went for

*Sarah learned to live with her father watching television late at night.*

the kids' rooms first," she says. "They'd gotten up and were as spooked as we were." Telling his wife to stay with the kids upstairs, Sara's husband rushed downstairs to investigate the crashing. "It didn't even occur to either of us to call the police."

Her husband had not yet reached the ground floor when chaos erupted. "Everything happened at once," says Sara. "The television in our bedroom turned on by itself at the highest volume, so loud we could hear the speakers cracking from my daughter's bedroom. The light in the hall started going on and off, like a strobe light, and we could hear footsteps, real heavy, going back and forth between the bedrooms, even though there was no one there." Above it all, she heard her husband, who had by this time reached the ground floor, shout, "Sweet Jesus!"

Sara acted quickly. "I felt right away that I knew what I had to do," she says. "I told my kids to stay put in the room, and shut the door behind me on my way out." From the hallway, the situation was worse than she had thought. "I passed the bathroom and could see the lights going on and off in there, too. The water was on all the way in the sink and the bathtub. There was a spot in the hall right outside our bedroom that was cold as anything."

But Sara did not pause. She continued straight downstairs to the living room, where she knew her husband would be. "He'd unlocked the doors and was in the doorway, looking in," Sara says. "I couldn't believe my eyes. The place was a complete mess. The sofa and love seat were on their sides, the coffee table and end tables were knocked over. We had two paintings hanging on the wall that looked like someone threw them across the room. Our table lamps were knocked over. The lights were flashing on and off. It was a complete disaster."

Before she had a chance to absorb what had been done, the television set they had moved into the office switched on by itself. They could hear it from down the hall. Like the television in their bedroom, it was blaring at full volume. An instant later, there was a crashing noise, as everything on the desktop was swept onto the floor. Sara and her husband arrived just in time to see their bulletin board launch off the wall and fly across the room.

"I thought it was obvious," Sara says. "Dad, or the thing that looked like Dad, was beside-himself-angry that we'd taken away the TV and chair. He was moving through the house, wrecking things, and the next room would be the kitchen." Yet as sure of that as she was, Sara's husband clearly wasn't on the same wavelength.

"When I started calling out that we were sorry for moving his things out of the living room, and would put everything back where it belonged double-quick, my husband looked at me like I'd turned into a ghost myself. He grabbed my arm and said something like: 'What the hell do you think you're doing?' I may as well have been one of the kids caught with their hands in the cookie jar. He just couldn't believe that I was trying to *talk* to it."

Seconds after she spoke, the house fell silent—the televisions turned off, the lights ceased their flickering, the water in the bathroom upstairs stopped running, and there were no more booming footfalls in the hallway between the bedrooms. "The main thing was that I needed to see that nothing happened in the kitchen, Sara says. "The thing that went through the living room could have made a right holy mess in that kitchen."

She says, "We weren't about to wait around for even one minute. I told my husband we were going to get that chair back from the garage and move the TV back into the living room."

Sara says that while her husband was not at all enthused about going to work in the middle of the night possibly to appease something that had just trashed their home, the matter that was not open for discussion. "Personally, I think it was a man thing," Sara laughs. "I guess I don't blame him, not wanting to make peace with a thing that wrecked your house. But what else do you do? How do you butt heads with a ghost? Simple—you don't."

Her husband did try to argue his point but didn't get far. "We didn't bother cleaning the living room up that night, but we set up the TV and put the armchair out in front of it. At that point, as long as it kept the volume down and didn't destroy my house, I was fine with it watching as much TV as it wanted."

Essentially, this resolution was about as close as Sara's family would come to the apparition. "It's still there," she says. "Every now and then on late nights, I'll see the light of the TV in the living room and know it's in there watching. It might sound crazy, but I don't even bother looking anymore. I just shut the doors in case the kids end up coming down." As much as she's tried to control her children's exposure to the apparition in the living room, they were already fully aware of the presence in the living room.

How does she explain it to her children? "By telling them that there are some things that we can't explain," Sara says. "I wasn't about to be dishonest, and I gave them the best answer I came up with for myself. I told them that their grandpa is gone, and that what they've seen in the living room isn't really him but a *part* of him. And that part wasn't ready to go yet and was holding on to the last thing he could remember—watching TV in the living room."

Sara says that when her children respond with the inevitable, "But why is Grandpa in pieces?" she goes no further. She assures them that what's happening is extremely unusual and offers the best advice she can think of. "I tell them that even though Mom can't say for sure what the thing that looks like Grandpa is, I can say for sure that they shouldn't go about telling everyone they know about it. Kids wouldn't get it and they'd just call my kids freaks. Living with a ghost is one thing, but when you have one kid in the fourth grade and another in seventh, being a 'freak' is a bigger deal."

# A Woman and her Pet

"Sebastian never was what you'd call a normal cat," says the anonymous Hampton resident who shall be called "Janet" for this story. "That rule about how cats are supposed to be all aloof and independent and don't give a squirt if you're around or not—well, over at cat headquarters, they forgot to give Sebastian that memo," she says with a snort. "On second thought, maybe someone got the memos mixed up and Sebastian got the one they gave all the dogs."

Janet claims she had always been more of a dog person, but her experience with Sebastian converted her into a cat person. "Probably 'cause Seb was such a damn dog to begin with. Ever since he was a kit, he'd follow me around where I went, and I mean really. I'd go to the washroom, and there was Seb, waiting outside by the door. I'm watching TV, he's on the couch. I'm eating dinner, and he's at my feet looking at me. The worst was when I'd go to work: the look he'd give me when I left the apartment broke my heart every morning, and you can bet when I got home he'd be all over me, purring away and rubbing himself against my leg. I gotta say, he was more dog than most dogs I know."

Taking into account the above, it was odd that Janet came to prefer cats over dogs after her experience with a cat that had serious canine traits. It was something she had to come to terms with after her beloved Sebastian died. "He wasn't 10 years old when he passed," Janet says, "and it was one hell of a thing to go through."

People do get attached to their pets, and in Janet's case, where she had gone through so many changes while in her cat's company, it felt as though her cat was her one constant during an unstable, insecure time in her life. "Me and Seb had gone through so much together," Janet says, "good and bad, highs and lows." She was living in a suburb outside of Alexandria when she picked up Sebastian as a kitten. She met her future husband shortly after adopting her cat, celebrating her cat's second birthday just before her marriage. Sebastian was only past four when she got divorced. After that, she moved five times in four years, quit three jobs and went back to school. Sebastian was there with her through it all, even 9/11: Sebastian was sleeping in her bed the morning she heard that terrorists had attacked the World Trade Center.

"I know it makes me sound crazy as a kook, but I was closer to my Seb than I was to most people in my life," Janet says. "One look and he knew when I was having a bad day. I had conversations with him all the time. Okay, well, not real conversations. They were pretty one-sided. Me ranting at the poor guy when things were lousy. I'd pretty well talk to him all the time like he was a real person. Like when something crazy was happening on the news, I'd tell him about how much of a mess we're making of this place, and you know, he'd *listen*. He'd sit there real still and give me this look with those green eyes of his. You'd swear that he could understand what I was on about."

When Janet woke up one December morning to find Sebastian lying lifeless at her feet, it was nothing less than a calamity. She says it was as though a part of her had been ripped away, and there was a time when she wondered if she would ever be the same. "I wasn't *half* that shaken up when I got my divorce," she says. "I could deal with anything. Whatever had been going on, me and Seb could deal with it.

But losing him, I almost couldn't deal with it. I missed work for over a week, didn't go out with anyone or do anything. I was a write-off."

Janet goes on to describe what can only be called severe depression. It was when things were darkest for her that the visitations began. "I was in bed the first time Seb came back," she says. "I'd been sleeping on and off all day, and when I woke up that time, it was about four in the morning, and I could feel the weight of Seb sleeping against my feet. I didn't even think about it for a few minutes. I was half asleep, and I was so used to Seb being there, years, I forgot that he died in the first place." For a dreamy, half-conscious moment, Seb was not dead, and everything was fine. Then Janet woke up.

"I went straight for the light," she says. "I was 50–50, half scared to death, half happier than anything." By the time she found the light switch, the feeling of Seb at her feet was gone. She was alone in her dimly lit bedroom. "I looked and looked that night—under the bed, behind the night tables, in the closets, kitchen cupboards. I looked everywhere. It was sense-less, and I knew it, but I also felt what I felt, and it seemed so *real*, that I was second-guessing my common sense, and even my memory for a sec: 'Did Seb *really* die?'"

Finally dismissing the incident as a dream, Janet went back to bed feeling, for the first time, some relief from the grinding grief of her loss. "I can't explain it, but things felt a little bet-ter that night," she says. "I didn't feel so all alone about it."

In fact, Janet has a theory that basic loneliness was at the root of her dilemma, exacerbating her grief. Even though people can understand profound depression at the loss of a family member or dear friend, it is much harder to accept such deep anxiety in a person whose pet dies. "Just get a new one!" Janet says. "That's what my mom told me. She didn't get it at all." Carrying the burden of her loss alone, Janet was also aware that it was not at all "normal" for her to be feeling the way she was. "There are a lot of people out there that would say my mom was right: just get a new one!"

Regardless, the encounter with her imaginary pet did her good. Two days later, she was back at work. It was her first shift in over eight days. "That same day, Seb came by to visit me again," Janet says. "There was this routine we had after I got back from work. I'd go straight to the washroom and he'd wait outside the door, scratching at it and sticking his paws underneath." Sebastian's absence must have loomed large after her first day back from work. Janet went to the washroom as she always did, though now there was no attention-starved cat at her heels. Or so she thought.

She says she did not even look up when the first set of claws scratched the door, assuming, without thinking, that she was hearing something else. But the scratching persisted, and suddenly it registered. "I looked down at the crack under the door and—would you believe it?—I saw the tips of Seb's little paws there," Janet says. "They were gray with white tips, just like his, and they were wiggling around all over the place, like he used to do."

Swinging open the door with incredulous hope, she looked down and saw nothing there. "I read somewhere that grieving folks sometimes hallucinate. They fool themselves into thinking that they're seeing whoever they lost." Janet told herself that was what was going on. She preferred to believe that she was hallucinating than that she was going insane, and at the time she did not believe she had any other options. But the coming days would change her mind.

"It wasn't like I was going, 'Hey! The ghost of my dead cat is back to stay with me!'" Janet says. "I was way more likely to say that I was going nuts. The ghost of a cat? Crazy. There was that Stephen King movie, *Pet Cemetery*, but who would think stuff like that actually happened?"

Quite a few, as it turns out. Phantom animals reoccur in paranormal literature. From manifestations of infamous black dogs in various countryside settings to favorite pets coming back from the dead to comfort their masters, experiences with ghostly dogs and cats are not so rare as some might assume.

"The next morning, I think, was the first time I really started thinking I might be dealing with Seb," Janet continues. "I was coming out of the shower. I grabbed the towel off the counter, where I always put my blankets, but when I went to move it, something else pulled on the other side." This "something else" pulling the blanket away was familiar to her. It had been one of Sebastian's habits to wait for her on the bathroom counter while she showered. Always attracted to the moving tassels sewn onto the corners of a few of her blankets, he always pounced and pulled back on them whenever Janet used them.

"That was too much. People might hallucinate their deceased loved ones, but I hadn't ever heard of people having tug of wars with them." The thought occurred to her for the first time: maybe it wasn't so crazy that Sebastian's ghost had come back to keep her company. Was it?

"I wasn't about to go out and buy him cat food at that point," she says. "Still, I'd be lying if I didn't say that was when things really started to change for the better for me. Maybe Seb was really still with me. Not in body, but in spirit. Why not?

We'd been through so much together." After that morning in the shower, the idea did not seem as crazy as she initially thought. Later, after work, Janet rushed home from work in the hopes that there would be yet another sign of her ghostly pet. She was not disappointed.

"That day, I heard him when I was in the hallway," she says. "He was meowing away on the other side when I was at the front door. I couldn't see him when I got inside, but it didn't matter. I knew he was there with me anyhow. I could *feel it*, as real as anything else."

Janet got used to having her phantom cat around. It was not the same as having the living, breathing version of her pet there, but it eased her grief and loneliness. "Things got better after I figured out that Seb was still around," she says. "A lot of people would probably be iffy about the whole thing, but I wasn't scared at all."

Janet took joy in the presence of her spectral pet, comforted by its regular appearances, and wondered at the new ways Sebastian would manifest himself. "There were some things that happened regular," Janet explains. "Like three, sometimes four times a week, I'd wake up early morning and feel Seb in bed, all warm against my feet." Other phenomena commonly occurred. Janet got used to having the ghost of her former pet playing with the tassels on her towels or scratching at the bathroom door. Every now and then, however, Seb would surprise her.

"There was one time when I came home from work and the toilet paper was completely unraveled in the bathroom. If he was still around, boy, I'd be mad, but how do you punish a ghost-cat?" Janet simply muttered, "Bad cat," into the air and went about cleaning up the mess. "A lot of the time, if you didn't shut the doors all the way, you'd know when Seb came into the room, 'cause the door would open up by itself." Janet's favorite was when the sound of heavy purring suddenly filled a room. "It didn't happen much," she says. "Usually, I'd be watching TV or eating dinner when it did. I never knew where Seb was purring from, but it made me happy to know he was in the room with me."

As far as appearances went, though, Janet's phantom cat proved to be quite elusive. "The only time I ever really *saw* him was when I was in the bathroom, and his little paws showed up under the door. Every time, I'd open that door as quickly as I could, but he was always gone. I could hear Seb, and sometimes I could feel him, but I never saw him." And neither did Janet's guests when she had them. "Seb was never a shy cat, but things were different now. He never came out when I had people over." This was probably a good thing. "I've got no clue what I would have said if he did start purring out of the blue in the middle of a visit."

Janet began thinking about getting another pet when she started to feel like herself again, not for a moment imagining that this would cause problems with Sebastian. "When I picked up Jules, I don't think I even *thought* about how he'd get along with Seb," Janet says. "First of all, Seb wasn't really around, the way other live animals are. For all I knew, I was the only one who could sense him. And, anyway, he never was the kind of cat that got into trouble with other animals when he was alive."

Janet quickly discovered that other animals related differently to him now that he was dead.

"The first few days Jules was with me went fine," she says. "He was a full-grown Russian blue that I took off a friend

who couldn't keep him anymore." Not suspecting any troubles, Janet cheerfully addressed Sebastian along with her new
cat. "I got silly about it, no question," she says. "I put out Seb's
water with Jules' bowl, and told Seb that he should come out
and say hi. I thought we could be a happy little family." That
was before she discovered that her new pet was not in love
with the idea of sharing a home with a ghost—even if that
ghost was a member of his species.

"They got in their first tussle about two weeks after I got
Jules," says Janet, "and it was one of the craziest things I've
ever seen." Until that night, Sebastian had been curiously
absent, not appearing once since Jules had arrived, a fact that
was starting to worry Janet. She was relieved when she woke
one morning with the familiar warmth pressed against her
feet. She had just managed to get out her whispered greeting
when chaos landed in the form of a battle-ready Russian blue
pouncing on her bed, claws extended, hissing.

"I'll just go on the record here to say that it's gotta be the
worst way to wake up—two cats fighting in your bed," Janet
says, laughing. "Especially when one of those cats is invisible
and can make the loudest noises you'd ever heard." It was a
violent scrap, if a single cat spinning and slashing against an
invisible, immaterial opponent qualifies as a scrap. "I couldn't
see Sebastian, but I could feel them both bouncing off the
bed. They were on the ground, and then Jules dashed out of
the room. I'm guessing he was still after Seb. Or else Seb was
after him, I can't really say which."

When Janet found Jules, he was crouched under her coffee
table, unwilling to come out no matter how he was coaxed.
"After that, things were pretty tense for a while," she says. "Seb
stopped coming out as much, and I'm pretty sure that it had

everything to do with Jules. Every now and then, I'd hear the cats screeching and hissing at each other; it got pretty loud sometimes."

The situation presented Janet with something of a problem. On one hand, she had already become attached to the stern-faced Jules. He did not share Sebastian's constant need for affection but carried himself with a kind of regal seriousness that she found adorable. Furthermore, there was the fact that he was actually alive. Yet even though Sebastian was no longer with her—materially, at least—even though he was invisible and only occasionally let her know he was present, she still had a deep bond with the cat that had, as she says, been with her through so much.

In the end, the situation resolved itself. "That spring, I got a job offer in Hampton that paid better, and I couldn't say no." Grateful as she was for the promotion, she was very sorry to move. "I knew that would be it for Seb," she says. "With Jules around, he was barely showing up anymore, anyway. I couldn't see him following us all the way to Hampton." In fact, for all Janet knew, he had already left in the weeks prior to the move. "The whole time I was boxing my things up, Seb didn't come around once." When time came to leave, Janet found herself unable to depart without leaving something behind for him just in case, and so she left behind his food and water bowl, both clean and full.

Looking back, Janet has a theory about the reappearance of her cat. "It probably sounds crazy," she says, "but then so is the situation. Personally, I think that Seb *knew* how bad it was for me after he was gone and came back to help me get back up on my feet." Such insight and compassion are much credit for a cat, dead or alive, but, according to Janet, Sebastian's plan did work. Things quickly began improving for her after the first morning she woke with his phantom body curled next to her.

Now she keeps a photograph of Sebastian on her living room wall, but has otherwise moved on, enjoying her time with the much more independent but no less loving Jules.

# Recently Departed

She is a Richmond nurse and she has a story to tell. "You see a lot of hard things working in an emergency room," she says. "I've done time in one of the biggest medical centers in the city—I'll just say that figuring out how to deal with it all was one of the toughest things. There's a lot of pain and sadness and people letting go. Sure, there's people fighting hard and getting better, too, but with a job like mine, you get used to dying. You see it enough."

Concerned with protecting her privacy and respecting the rights of others, our nurse requests that all places and names in her story be left out. The name she takes here, "Anna Stevens," is fictional, and her patient, her friend and the hospital in which she works shall not be named. Regardless, these details are secondary to her story.

"This happened about two years ago," Nurse Stevens begins. "He was suffering a heart attack when he came in, and we couldn't save him. I won't say anything about this man's condition other than he was an old man and had a history of heart problems. You could say about him that he lived a full life and that it was his time, as much as it ever is anybody's."

When Stevens discovered who had been waiting for this man, his passing became immediately more personal. "I recognized her right away, when the doctor was telling her that her husband was gone. She was my English teacher from high school. She looked a lot older but really still the same. I remembered her right off because she was one the best teachers I ever had, and also because she became friends with my parents. After I graduated, they would have her and her husband over for dinner every now and again. Sometimes they would go see movies. I saw her occasionally after high school, and always talked for a few minutes whenever she was over. Then I moved out and she and my parents drifted apart, and that was it. I hadn't really thought about her in years."

But then there she was—receiving news of her husband from her former student. "It got to me that I must have met this man a few times, but when he came in, he didn't look familiar at all. I mean that, until I saw my old English teacher, I'd forgotten about him altogether." As she approached her former high school teacher to offer her condolences, memories about the man came back, small details—the lambskin leather jacket he wore, the deep smile lines, what she read as contentment in his then middle-aged face.

Stevens continues: "She recognized me right off, too. I said hello and hugged her and she cried, but only a little. It hadn't sunk in for her yet. I knew it was hard for her, but she's such a nice lady. She wanted to know about my family and me. She hadn't spoken with my folks since they moved out of Richmond. English was my best subject in high school, and she was surprised I went into nursing. She was asking how long I'd been a nurse and if I was married and so on."

By the time the two of them parted, they had made promises to see each other again sometime soon. "I gave her my phone number and told her to call me anytime for lunch or if she just wanted to talk. I knew it wasn't one of those fake things, either. I knew I'd be hearing from her again."

Just two days later Stevens was on the phone with her. "I was surprised for sure," she says. "She hadn't had the funeral yet, and honestly, at the time, I didn't feel close enough to even attend it. I guess I was surprised that she didn't want to spend time with people who were closer." Stevens pauses before emphasizing a point. "Thing is, I was surprised, sure, but I wasn't *too* surprised. People grieve in their own ways, and I was glad to see her, even though the situation was terrible. I'd say we've become friends since then, but let me tell you—it ended up being a crazy way to get reacquainted."

Meeting her old teacher in a restaurant for lunch, Stevens could see right away that she was having a hard time. "She was distracted and nervous, and she looked like she hadn't slept since I saw her," she recalls. "She was in no mood to eat, and we ended up canceling food and going for a walk instead."

They were walking along the James River when the former teacher finally spoke. "She hadn't said two words on our way out there, and I'm quiet, giving her time to open up. Then, first thing comes out is: 'How do I look to you? Do I seem all right? Anything about me strike you as crazy? Do I seem crazy?'"

Stevens tried humor. "I told her that I worked in the ICU, not Psych, so crazy wasn't my specialty. But, no, she looked fine, considering what she was going through and all." The conversation took a strange turn soon after that, when Stevens learned why her teacher had called her.

She told Stevens then that she needed to talk to someone about what she had been going through. The problem was that she could not tell anyone she knew too well, or anyone who had been close to her husband. "She said she thought it'd be too painful for the people she knew. That they'd get worried, thinking she was going nuts, and she told me she knew some people who'd even get a bit upset if she opened up about what had been going on."

The Richmond nurse understood why when the grieving woman finally told her what was on her mind. "It was her husband," Stevens says. "She told me that her husband had been appearing next to her in bed both nights since he's passed. She needed to talk to somebody about it, because as happy as she was to see him, she was also saying that it was impossible and that she was scared. She thought that maybe she was losing her mind."

Anna Stevens did not think so. "It happens to people dealing with grief," she says, "where they're convinced that they've seen and sometimes even spoken to people they've lost." Assuming that was what was happening, she assured her friend that such a thing was not unusual, and that it was quite common for grieving individuals to experience such hallucinations. "On top of it, she was in bed when she saw him. I tried suggesting that it was even likely that she was half asleep and dreamt it."

But as Stevens was trying to comfort her, telling her that she did not think there was any cause for concern, she could see that it was going to take more than words to put the older woman's mind at ease. "I knew what she was going to ask before she asked it. She wanted me to spend a night at her place, to see if he would show up again and if I could see him."

It was quite the request, especially coming from someone Stevens really hardly knew. How did she feel about it? "I thought it was weird, for sure. I couldn't understand at first why she couldn't ask someone who knew them both, but when I thought about it some more, it made more sense. Calling up someone and asking to look out for a ghost of a friend who just died two days ago, that isn't the kind of call anyone would want to make."

Stevens agreed to join the grieving widow that night. The plan was that she would sleep in the guest room with her cell phone on the night table. If the woman's husband arrived, she was to call Stevens' cell phone, and Stevens would run up to the bedroom to either confirm or contradict what her friend was seeing.

"Call it the skeptic in me, but I didn't really think anything was going to happen," Stevens says. "Then again, call it the analytic mind in me, but when I showed up at her place, I had a little automatic camera stashed in my bag." Stevens does admit that, while her friend was telling her the story, she was asking herself why the woman did not just take a camera to bed herself. If she caught the apparition of her husband on film, she would get the same validation. "But then that's pretty clear-cut thinking," she says, "and you've got to appreciate that a woman who lost her husband two days ago isn't going to be thinking so clear-cut."

Stevens did not really expect anything to happen at her friend's house that night, did she? Was she expecting to see a ghost? "God, no. It was all about helping out this great lady who was having a bad time. Sure, I brought my camera, but that was just that little 'come-prepared' voice acting in my head. I didn't believe in a million years I'd be using it trying to take a picture of a ghost."

Even when she was woken by the sound of her cell phone ringing later that night, Stevens did not believe she was going to see anything but a scared woman in a darkened bedroom. Still, as she groggily rose from bed, she remembered to take the camera with her.

"I still get chills when I think about it," she says. "Her bed-room door was open, and I walked in without saying any-thing, which was what she told me to do 'cause she didn't want to take the chance that I'd scare him away." She could make out the bed, but not much else, in the darkness of the bedroom, so she walked in quietly, her camera dangling around her wrist. "I was about, I don't know, five feet from the bed when it got really, really cold. I'm talking it was ice-box cold in the space around her bed. I was getting goose-bumps up and down my body, and was wondering what the hell was going on." Despite her growing unease, Stevens was still fishing for rational explanations, wondering if there was a directed air conditioner that had been running for too long.

"All that went out the window when I saw that there were two shapes in the bed," she says. "I think I froze for a good minute at least. It was dark in there, and I wasn't sure if I could believe my eyes, but I could see this…*man*, lying right beside her. He was on his back, with his arms at his side, look-ing straight up at the ceiling."

Stevens' former English teacher broke the silence. "Can you see him?" she whispered.

"It took a little for me to register what she asked. I think I just said, 'That's him.'" Stevens says it was all she could get out. A strange paralysis had seized her, and she felt it growing stronger with every second she stood and stared. "The best way I can describe it is it was like ice water in my veins, like the cold was moving through my body, from my chest out to my head and extremities. All I could do was stand and stare."

The older woman asked Stevens if she was carrying her camera. All the nurse could do was nod, still transfixed by the sight of the man in front of her, whom she knew in her bones was not alive. "I guess she'd gotten used to him," Stevens says with a laugh, "because she took over pretty quick. She had to tell me twice to snap a damn picture before it registered."

Standing there mouth agape, Stevens turned on her camera, raised it to her face and clicked the shutter. "The flash lit the bed up for a second, and by that light I could see he wasn't there anymore," she says. The extreme cold by the bed had also gone, and it was now just the two women in the bedroom.

"I never spent another night over at her place," Stevens says, "but if she asked me, I would have. Imagine having your dead husband coming into your room at night. No one should have to deal with that on their own." Nevertheless, all the former English teacher seemed to want was confirmation that the apparition of her husband existed outside her own mind, and once Stevens provided that, she was okay.

"I went and got that photo developed the next day," Stevens says, "but it was just a picture of one side of a queen-sized bed, just like what I saw when the flash went." She later learned that, though he vanished that night, he did return later that night and for two more nights after that. Only after his funeral, after his remains were buried, did he cease the nightly visits with his wife.

"It's been about two years now, and she hasn't seen him since," Stevens says. "I've become close with her since then, and we don't talk about that night too much anymore. But every now and then, when she's talking about some trip she took with her husband, or a restaurant she used to go to with him, I know we're both thinking about that night."

It was a common experience that had a significant effect on both women's outlook. On the last night he appeared,

Stevens' friend was able to say goodbye to her husband, an opportunity she was grateful for. Stevens found herself reassessing the way she looked at life and death. "I'd been around mortality a lot, but I'd never seen any, and I mean *any* evidence of life, of *anything*, after death. Scary as the whole experience was, I'm glad I went through it now. It's given me…" Nurse Stevens takes a moment before she finishes, "you could say it's given me faith."

# 4

# Other
# Eerie
# Tales

# In the Appalachian Shadows

For three years it was something of a miniature invasion—
George Hart and a gang of his Pennsylvania school chums
would descend onto the woods of the Virginia Appalachians
after final exams. There they would make merry in fine post-
academic fashion with as much alcohol and tomfoolery as
they could manage. "We started going down—I guess you
could call it a tradition—in freshman year, so it got about as
stupid as you can imagine," Hart says. "We brought down all
the booze we could carry, and as many as three to four cars of
guys with a hell of a lot to celebrate."

The destination was always the same, a Bath County campsite within the vast woodlands of the George Washington
National Forest. The group had been made aware of it by one
of the revelers' older brothers, who had belonged to a group
who had likewise taken to descending on the campsite in the
wake of their exams. "You could say we were keeping tradition alive," Hart laughs. "It was a party with a purpose—the
worst kind, right?"

This is the former Pennsylvania student's tone—remi-
niscence with that brand of nostalgia that is the preserve
of young men talking about past drinking escapades. But a
queer little detail emerges quickly after the blithe "party with
a purpose." "The whole thing started in the first place because
my buddy's older brother told everyone there was a witch in
those parts. He said she was somewhere in the woods around
that campsite, that he saw her himself when he went camping
there in high school.

"It was some trip with a bunch of friends and their dads. At night, these kids got to talking about a story that one of the fathers told before they went to bed, about how there was a witch right around there. You know, the Appalachian witch— a crazy old woman who lives in the forest, stays away from people, wears animal skins, prays to the Devil and eats children—the sort of things that get people's blood up around the campfire.

"Well, it's nighttime and every noise outside their tent is the witch crawling around, right? So this guy, the one who started up the whole tradition of going down there, went out into the woods on a dare, and he saw her. All he had was his flashlight, but he saw her face for a second or two. Right ugly, dirty and mean-looking, all hunched up with a walking stick in one hand, moving quick through the trees."

It is very likely that none of the students took the story too seriously, assuming that the teller was either pulling their legs, or—considering that he never recanted the story—had simply been seeing things. In the end, the tale provided a great setting for their end-of-the-year celebration. Their outing became the annual "witch hunt," where blowing off steam was the main objective, with a whisper of ominous promise. As long as the purported eyewitness never went back on his story, there was always a hint of fear, an unspoken thrill, when someone brought up the witch after the sun went down.

"We heard a lot of stories from the guys before us," Hart says. "About how, one time, one guy got up to take a leak late at night and felt something that he swore was human brush past him. Another time, there were two other guys going for a bit of a hike; they came back talking about how they heard someone cackling in the woods—real witch-like, of course.

These were just too obvious, and the guys who told them were real jokers. None of us took them too seriously. But there were a few stories that were actually kind of spooky—made you think a bit.

"Like this one guy, more serious than the others, didn't kid around so much. I guess one night he saw a light going up and down the outside of their tent. Then he heard something moving out there, something big that came right up against his tent and started sniffing. He said that when the light moved over the animal he could see the shadow of a big dog on his tent. Well, just when he was getting really freaked out, the guy heard someone's voice call the dog, it sounded like 'Hunter,' and the dog went running back at the same time as the light vanished. He said he didn't hear the voice too clearly. He said it sounded hard and rough but swore that it was a woman."

With such accounts coming from the mouths of relatively reliable individuals, the thrill of the Appalachian witch persisted over the years. The guys were definitely not going on this annual camping trip because they *believed* in the witch, but there was just enough doubt that, on certain nights, the darkness in the woods could acquire a certain amount of daring.

Hart and his friends were after this thrill, along with the pursuit of excessive drink, the last time they headed south for the Virginian Appalachians. "There were only five of us that year," he recalls. "Way less than there'd been in times before, but that didn't bother anyone too much."

The weekend began as it had the previous two years. They arrived at the campsite in the early afternoon, unpacked, set up and almost immediately proceeded to get drinking. As usual, they were pretty well the only ones in the secluded campground. "I was out early that first night," says Hart, confessing that he always needed sleep the first night if he hoped to keep up with his hard-drinking peers for the rest of the weekend. That meant he would be the first one up, too.

That was what he assumed. Much to his surprise, one of Hart's friends was already awake when he got up. "It was especially weird, 'cause this guy, Jeff, was one of the craziest. He should've just gotten to sleep, not be the first person up." It turned out that Jeff had not slept at all, and not because he was having too much fun, either.

"He didn't say anything at first—stayed pretty well quiet when I was making breakfast and going on about what he was doing up. It took a few minutes, but when I finally looked at the guy, it was obvious that there was something wrong. Like, he looked pretty out of it." Hart stopped his patter and his cooking and asked Jeff what was the matter.

"He kind of laughed at first. That's the kind of guy he is. But it was a pretty weak show. So then he looks at me, all serious, and he says, 'You hear anything last night?'"

It suddenly clicked. "Right away, I'm thinking, *Really? The witch? Is he kidding?* I made some crack, something stupid about low-flying broomsticks, but he wasn't into it. He was trying to be cool about the whole thing, but it was pretty obvious that there was a problem."

Hart says his friend got bolder then. "He asked me again. He says, 'No joke. You didn't hear anything?'"

It didn't seem possible to Hart where his friend was going with this. Not knowing how to react, he fell back on humor again. But Jeff still wasn't laughing. He finally submitted to hearing the story his friend so obviously wanted to tell.

"As usual, Jeff was the last guy awake," Hart says. "He told me he just stopped drinking a few hours back, and was still kind of plastered. Everyone was passed out, and it was about six-ish when he got into his tent. He's drunk and tired as all hell, and is about to totally black out when he hears these footsteps. Now he's awake, bugging out, wondering who the hell's in our campsite. He hears the footsteps getting closer and this grunting, huffing noise; it sounds like a person. After a minute or two, he gets up the nerve to ask who's out there. Whatever's outside the tent stops moving, and there's no more grunting and huffing. It's real quiet. He can't say for sure how long it's like that, then he says he hears this voice out of nowhere, like it's right up against his tent, this hoarse, whispering voice. He isn't sure, but it sounds like 'Kids ain't no more 'round here.' Ugly as the voice was, he swore it was a woman's."

Unable to sleep for the rest of the night, Jeff remained tucked away in his one-man tent, crawling out only when the sun's early light was visible. George Hart found him a few hours later, bleary eyed and frightened, replaying the incident over and over in his mind.

"I think you've got to know Jeff to get why we all reacted the way we did," Hart says. "He's the guy with all the stories. Get enough booze in him, and that's all you need for entertainment. If he isn't spewing some bogus, over-the-top tirade, then he's break dancing without any clothes on. He's always the first one to start drinking and the last one to call it a night. Basically, a great guy to have around for a party, but not the sort of person you'd ever take too seriously. It couldn't have worked out better that Jeff, of all people, was the one who heard the supposed whispering."

No one thought for a second to take him seriously, and the wisecracks were coming all day. Hart and his friends took immense joy in the fact that Jeff heard the witch whispering to him while he was in a drunken stupor. Funny as it was to them, the fact that he had taken it so seriously made it even richer. The three other campers asked Hart to describe Jeff's subdued demeanor over and over throughout the day, laughing just as hard each time. The snickering, says Hart, went something like: "Leave it to Jeff to get so drunk that he's got witches whispering to him in his tent." Later on that night, however, it would not seem nearly so funny.

"Jeff slept through a lot of the day, so we had a lot to throw at him by the time he got up," Hart says. "We were still going strong by the time the sun started to go down, all about what she'd say to Jeff this time around." As the sky darkened, they got a fire going, put some music in the portable stereo and began with the ritual alcohol consumption.

"I can't say what time it was when things started to get weird," Hart says. "All I can say for sure is that it was sometime past quarter after one, because that was when my watch froze." Hart discovered his watch had stopped while he was heading out to go to the bushes for a bathroom break. It had been dark for quite some time, and he was using a flashlight to guide himself. "As soon as I got away from everyone and was by myself in those woods, things felt different," he says. "It was like, suddenly Jeff's story wasn't so funny. My head starts fooling with me—I'm imagining what I'd do right then if I heard a rough woman's voice whisper in my ear." It was then, after he'd finished, that Hart looked at his watch and saw that it had stopped. It was sometime past quarter after one, and things were about to take a decidedly terrifying turn.

"I was heading back, walking quicker than normal for sure because at this point, I'm bona fide bugging out. I think it went like this: me thinking how crazy it would be if there was an old lady somewhere in these woods, then *hearing* someone walking along behind me." With his heart suddenly tickling his tonsils, Hart turned to see if there was anybody behind him. There, barely visible in the near-total darkness of the trees, was an even darker silhouette.

"Damn right scared out of my mind is how I'd describe it," Hart says. "I swung my flashlight over to see better and started to run. I think I shouted, 'Who's there?' or something like that." Whatever he asked, he didn't get an answer. And he didn't get too far, either. His flashlight had flickered and died an instant before he was able to shine it on the figure he thought he had seen. He just caught an image for a second, revealed in the light's dim periphery. He lost his footing as he ran and tumbled to the ground.

"I could hear the music playing and the guys laughing," Hart says, "and it was funny the first thing that popped into my head was that I wasn't going to start shouting. I couldn't lose it. Really, it was the middle of the night, and we were in the middle of the woods. If I started blubbering and shouting about how I swore I just saw the witch—that she was right here, right now—everyone being drunk as they are, who knows how crazy things would get. I remember I was thinking: *No matter what, stay calm.*"

Instead, Hart jumped to his feet as fast as he was able and began to run in the direction of the campfire and the voices. He had not taken a dozen steps when the tone of those voices abruptly changed. "First everyone went quiet," he says. "Then

I hear one of the guys go, 'What the hell was that?' And then, right after that, the music goes out."

There were curses and complaints when the boom box went out, and Hart's friends were crowded around the machine when he came running into the clearing, dead flashlight in hand, heart pounding away, doing his best to remain calm. "I remember how hard it was to keep my head when I started talking," he says. "First thing I did was get as close to the fire as I could. And then I pretty well told them, real calm and serious-like, that there was someone in the woods."

The buzz around the boom box ceased instantly. "What do you mean there's someone in the woods?" one of Hart's friends said, obviously uneasy.

Jeff, looking especially frightened, joined Hart by the fire. "You saw her?" was all he said.

"I think there was a few minutes when no one was ready to take me seriously," Hart says. "One buddy, Ryan, even went on like he didn't hear me—kept fiddling with the stereo. He took the batteries out and went looking for a fresh pack in his car." There was a pause before the other two campers quietly stepped forward so they were closer to the light of the campfire.

The question was repeated: "What do you mean there's someone in the woods?"

"I told them what happened—about the footsteps and how my flashlight went out, but I still saw her for a second."

What did she look like? When Hart is asked this question today, he pauses for a long moment. "Well," he finally offers, "I only saw her for a second before the flashlight died on me, and what I did see was pretty dim. Like I said, I only got her in the edge of my light. Maybe in a way, though, that made it worse. You know, in a bright room, she'd probably just look like a scraggly old lady that spent too many days in the woods without cleaning herself, but the way she looked that night, it still gets to me when I think about it.

"For starters, she was short, real short. She looked sort of hunched over. Her head looked huge, but I think most of it was her hair. It was big and gray and all over the place. A lot of it was hanging over her face, so I couldn't really see her eyes, but what I could see of her face wasn't pretty. Her skin was dirty, and I could make out these big, I don't know, *growths*, around her mouth."

Hart's description comes with a definite disclaimer. "When I think back, though, I've got to say that it's hard to separate what I actually saw from what I may have…imagined. I say this because the picture in my head is pretty crazy. I know that I didn't have any time to get a good look at her, but when I think of the picture in my head now she's even got pointy teeth, which, really, has got to be impossible. Why would a witch file down her teeth? That's seriously taking it too far in the evil department, isn't it?"

Hart cannot recall how many of these details he divulged to his friends, but whatever he said was enough to cast a tense silence over the campsite—a silence that was about to be shattered by outright panic.

"We all just about lost it when the radio came on," he says. "The thing just switched on by itself. It was 'Back in Black' at full blast, and the CD was skipping all over the place. Ryan was the closest guy to the stereo, and he was looking at it like it was the anti-Christ or something." Hart says it took him a few seconds to realize why. "I saw that he was carrying a fresh pack of batteries in his hands, and the batteries that were in before were on the ground. It was running with no batteries."

A riot of shouts and swears erupted from the five campers as Ryan ran forward to switch off the stereo, if such a thing was possible. It wasn't. "There was this minute or two, I think, where everything went nuts. Ryan was banging on the stereo, trying to get it to stop, and everybody was talking all sorts of nonsense at once."

Then, out of the corner of his eye, Hart saw her. "She was standing at the edge of the light, right at the edge of the trees, so I couldn't see her too clearly—just the scraggly outline of her head and her bent-over shoulders. I don't know if I imagined it or not, but it seemed to me that she was smiling with these long, pointed teeth."

The campsite quickly went quiet when the stereo finally stopped blaring the skipping AC/DC song. All eyes were on the stereo and their panting friend standing next to it. They looked at one another, then, silently. Hart was distracted for a moment. "I remember looking over at Jeff and him going, 'Holy crap.' Then when I looked back at where she'd been standing, there was nobody there anymore."

The incident effectively concluded the revelry. They spent the rest of the night in subdued conversation, jumping at every sound in the forest, the stereo locked away in one of the car trunks. "They kept asking me what happened when I was out in the woods, about what she looked like," Hart says, "and I didn't hold anything back. But, that night, I didn't say a word about how I saw her again when the stereo was blaring. Things were screwed up enough as it was. Last thing I wanted to do was make it worse."

Hart eventually told everyone weeks later about how she had appeared near the campsite—when they had acquired enough distance, when the night in the woods was no longer the sole topic of conversation. "When I think about it now, I'm surprised about how easy it was to get on with life as usual," he says. "It was like everyone decided they had enough of it. No one really seemed to care too much anymore, or else pretended not to. Except for Jeff. He couldn't get enough about her. He called me up a few times after that to talk about it, what happened. We'd end up talking about it for a while, going on about how much we thought about it, going over the details over and over, just in case there was something we left out. We wondered if we should tell anybody about it."

The last consideration was actually contrary to what the whole group had previously agreed on. They made this resolution while waiting for the sun to rise on that frightful night in the woods. "We all agreed on two things," Hart says. "One, that we wouldn't tell anybody about what happened, and two, that we were all done with camping out there. No more Virginia next year. It was pretty obvious that whatever was out there in those woods didn't want us around."

They have stuck to the latter resolution. Although they did have one last year-end celebration after that last camping trip, it was a far less ambitious affair, taking place in a local bar instead. The other resolution has obviously been broken. "It's funny how it ended up," Hart says. "We didn't talk about what happened too much at first, but then after a while it crept back, but something happened. It became a bit of a joke. Like if we were sitting around having drinks, we started making cracks about the whole thing. Maybe having a laugh over the look on whoever's face when the whole thing was going down, or else making cracks about how it was whoever's mother or girlfriend coming after us. A lot of people ended up hearing these cracks."

Hart says that, as far as he knows, none of them has spoken seriously about what occurred that night. Humor has been their way of coping. "It's easy enough to kid about it," he says, "but I get the feeling it'd be hard to get most of those guys to talk seriously. It's just not something that would happen.

"All I know is that I'm not about to piss off or embarrass any of the guys. I know that none of them would be willing to talk about it frankly like this. And too bad at that, 'cause it's a hell of a story, isn't it?"

# The Ghostly Caverns of the Shenandoah

A digging crew was laboring under the earth in Rockbridge County. They worked with pick axes, shovels and dynamite, these rough men with grimy faces and thick necks. They were pragmatic, unsentimental men used to underground spaces, so they did not notice the natural splendor surrounding them—a cascading waterfall, a huge lake of the clearest water, a massive domed cave bristling with ancient stalactites. They were unfazed by the wonders of Buck Hill Cavern, fixed on the job they'd been hired to complete—constructing a 275-foot entrance into the belly of this subterranean spectacle.

It was midday, though no one down below noticed—the brutish cadence of their labor was undisturbed by pause or conversation. Then, from somewhere in the darkness ahead, there was a sound. It was barely audible over the measured crash and bang of the dig, but each of them heard it, and they stopped. The sudden stillness was all the more silent for the cacophony that preceded it. The workers stared into the darkness ahead, dimly illuminated by the thin line of lanterns along the wall. No one spoke for a long moment. Then: "Did you hear that?"

There was another extended silence before the response. "Sure did."

One of the young diggers took a step forward, pick axe hanging loose at his side. "What the hell was it? And why has it gotten so cold all of a sudden?"

"Quiet down," said gruff voice, timbre heavy with authority. There was the crunch of his boots, then his enormous silhouette on the wall; he stood by the frightened digger. "Probably something collapsed up ahead. No need to go wettin' yer pants."

Even as he spoke, though, the man in charge felt there was something wrong. The boy was right; there was a bizarre chill in the air. No—it wasn't in the air. It was as if there was a chill within, numbing his bones, crawling up his back. He had been moiling beneath the earth for a long time and had never felt such a thing. He knew by the silence that the men around him were thinking the same.

Then the job took over. He thought of his meeting with Colonel Henry Parsons, the owner of the cave. The scheme was to clear out the entrance they were digging so that the public—that is to say, the paying public—would have access to the wonders beneath. His outfit had a job to do: build this tunnel. And no little noise in the dark was going to stop them.

He turned to his paralyzed diggers. "All right, you worthless dirt bags, I don't give a damn who thinks he heard what. This hole ain't gonna dig itself. Now get to work!"

No sooner had the order left his mouth than a long, tortured moan sounded from down the cave.

"What the hell?" Someone dropped his shovel. The footsteps of another digger were heard over stone and water, running for the surface.

"Get back here!" roared the boss. But an instant later there was another long moan that was closer than before. Everyone felt it, like an actual physical cold up their backs, down their arms.

When the moan sounded again, it was so close it could have been yards away in the darkness just beyond their sight. "Tommyknockers!" someone shouted.

"Tommyknockers? Children's stories, you weak-kneed idiots!" shouted the boss, though fear had now worked its way into his fury. *Tommyknockers?* The thought, unwanted, came. *Little goblins living underground, comin' out to scare the livin' Jesus out of folk?* He'd worked on countless digs, descended into more mines than he cared to remember. Never once did he ever see or hear anything that would give credence to such a legend. But now, under the wild old verdure of the Shenandoah Valley, there was something up in the darkness ahead, and half his men were running back for the surface. And now, the cold dread in his own veins was telling him to do the same.

There was the moan again, closer even than before. Two more men bolted, the rest standing clustered behind the boss. Then there was movement, a dark outline against one of the walls, and that was it. Each and every one of them turned and ran, as fast as their heavy legs would take them—the boss leading the way.

So ended the dig of 1889, and Colonel Henry Parsons' hopes at making some money out of the natural treasure that was Buck Hill Cavern. No matter how much he was willing to beg, flatter or bribe, the digging crew would not go back down, and as word spread fast about the thing at the bottom of Buck Hill, no one else was willing to venture down, either. It was not for another 90 or so years that the job was resumed and, this time, completed. Colonel Henry Parsons was right. In came the tourists, thousands upon thousands yearly, eager to catch a glimpse of the famous caves of the Virginia Appalachians. From Weyer's Cave in the northern part of Augusta County down to the Skyline Caverns in

*Do spirits still wander deep within these caverns?*

Warren, nature beneath the Shenandoah was just as much of an attraction as the scenic beauty above.

Yet as much as tourists value these underground sites today, a number of early Virginians could not get far enough away from them. True, there were always those who admired the caves for their beauty, as many people today do. Thomas Jefferson, who once owned areas of the Shenandoah, was known to brag about the beauty of these caves. Likewise, explorers marveled at them when they stumbled upon them, and local writers were never in short supply of effusive prose when ruminating on them. Still, the caverns in the western part of the state have been subjected to their share of negative press.

In general, folklore through the ages and across cultural lines has given underground settings a bad reputation. Some of the earliest myths locate Hades in his Underworld, while malicious goblins and greedy dwarves likewise have been said to burrow under the earth to make their homes. And, of course, there's the burning pit of fire and brimstone that needs little introduction or elaboration.

Is it any wonder, then, that early Americans were generally spooked when stumbling on the Appalachian caverns? As it was, these lands were strange enough to the new occupiers, inhabited as they were by a people with customs that were different from their own. It would not take much for these often-fearful pioneers to attribute evil to the dark, dank caverns they found when they ventured west.

Tales abounded. There was the story about the cursed cavern, where a young man discovered a skeleton while exploring it. Thinking a skull would make a nice ornament for his home, the explorer removed the head and took it back with him. Of course, the spirit that once resided in the old bones preferred its skull to remain above its collarbone, and so off it went after the interloper who had taken his head. The young man was harassed night and day by his supernatural tormentor until he got the idea of putting the skull back in the cave where he found it. The ghost bothered him no more.

This legend wasn't the only one to emerge from Virginia's caverns. Native American ghosts drifted at wooded entries to the caves, Tommyknockers abused unsuspecting miners and evil spirits did plain old evil things. Simply put, to many of these early Virginians, underground was unknown or unfamiliar, and unknown or unfamiliar was generally suspected to be bad. That thinking might account for the bizarre tales that involve the caverns.

And yet, these bizarre tales were hardly limited to early settlers in the region. In fact, the presence at the bottom of Buck Hill Cavern seems to have survived through the years. The men who were employed by Colonel Parsons were not the only ones who had a run-in with the thing that dwells below. Just like those 19th-century diggers, many visitors to Buck Hill throughout the late 1900s claimed to hear bone-chilling moans in the darkness. It has been written that visitors have encountered the moans of the subterranean entity—or entities—at different times in 1978, 1980,1985 and 1988.

Unlike Colonel Parsons' diggers, apparently, none among these eyewitnesses suspected mischievous Tommyknockers were responsible for these sounds. Unable to get behind the idea of wicked little gremlins living under the earth, contemporary eyewitnesses instead seem more receptive to the idea of one or a number of tortured spirits residing in the caverns, though who these spirits are, and what exactly they are tortured by, remains a mystery.

# The Devil Dog

It has been said that, in some parts of Virginia, the Devil will occasionally take it upon himself to visit certain individuals who are on their deathbeds. To merit such attention from the Dark Prince himself, these individuals would have been especially wicked souls throughout their lives. The earthly actions of these men and women were so vile, so heinously pernicious, that none in the community has any doubt about where they'll be toasting their toes in the afterlife. It is these individuals who, as they breathe their last, get the dubious pleasure of a formal welcome to the rest of their eternity by none other than Lucifer himself, *aka* Satan. The form he takes? The Devil Dog.

This account comes from the westernmost point of the state of Virginia, somewhere in Lee, Wise or Scott County, sometime before the Civil War. It is said that there was a Virginian who was fully and completely, undeniably and unforgivably reprehensible. Born wealthy, he was an inveterate lay-about. He made a practice of casually killing his slaves for nothing more than sport. He reportedly refused them a proper burial, once telling one or two of his field slaves to put his victim in the ground whenever they had time away from their other tasks.

What's more, this brute was married no less than five times, each time to a virtuous and wealthy woman who fell mysteriously ill and died shortly after being wed. With each woman's demise, he grew wealthier. Whether he murdered slaves for his entertainment or wives for their money, this man always gained from the demise of others. It was a pattern that repeated itself over and over through the course of his life. It was just his way. And he was hated for it.

But no matter how much luxury he lived in, no matter what his wealth, he, like all people, would eventually have to come to terms with his own mortality. For such a man as he, there was no coming to terms. Despite all his terrible earthly actions, he had grown to be a believer and knew for certain that he was doomed. He had already been judged. Hellfire waited.

He had no idea how right he was. One day he became too sick to care for himself, and his neighbors came to prepare his deathbed. They put out crisp white sheets and did what they could to ease the man's passing. By all accounts, he took his time. Wheezing and coughing, he held on to life longer than anyone thought possible, clutching his bedposts and holler-ing at the ceiling that he would not go without a fight.

The old man challenged God to come down and show Himself, so that he might get a better look at who was rob-bing him of everything he had. For those who were look-ing after him, this was high drama, watching the wicked old man rail against his mortal bonds. After all, he was one of the region's most powerful men, and some people began to wonder if the Almighty might indeed make a showing for this man's benefit. Sinful as he was, he had risen in wealth and rank. His caretakers grew increasingly uneasy at the mouth-frothing invective, the taunts, the sacrilegious rants coming from this vile, wholly iniquitous man who was determined to remain alive. Surely the Almighty would not let it pass with-out response. If He would not come down to address this vile dying man, then someone among His angelic host, a divine messenger, gleaming and terrible, could put this sinner in his place.

In the end, a messenger did come, but it was not from God, and it did not say a single word. It came around midnight, when the man's furious litany had become a tired drone. His health had deteriorated rapidly, and no one was expecting him to make it through the night. It was quiet in the old man's chamber. All the caretakers sat still, hushed at the now inevitable passing. If indeed there was going to be some sort of divine response, it would have to come soon because he would not be alive much longer.

The silence was broken by a sound outside the door. Something was shuffling down the hall, sniffing under the door, scratching at the threshold. At that moment, everyone in the room was overcome by dread—a preternatural terror that seized them. They all turned to the door, even the old man. He quit his muttering and sat up, staring wide-eyed at the entrance. His voice was low when he said, "So he's finally come."

But it was no messenger from God that came into the room. One more hard scratch at the door and it swung open. There, at the threshold, was an enormous black dog. The biggest animal any of them had ever seen, it stood over four feet high at the shoulders, with a coal-colored coat and eyes of fire—the color of the setting sun.

It looked at no one but the old man as it padded into the room, its burning stare fixed hungrily on the emaciated Virginian. He had been concocting elaborate diatribes against his maker for the last several days, but now he was only able to produce one word: "No."

His bitter eloquence instantly dissolved. "No, no, no, no," he repeated, over and over, a terrified mantra of denial. Still the beast came, indifferent to the old man's pleas. When it reached the foot of his bed, it reared up on its hind legs, standing now taller than a man, casting its fierce gaze down upon the bed.

"Help me! Help me! It's the Devil come to take me!" His cries were the horrible lamentations of a man standing before damnation. The dog stood fast, and none dared lift a hand against it. It did not move but only watched as the man thrashed in bed, trying to free himself of the sheets and escape his deathbed. He never made it. His heart stopped and he slumped lifeless on his bed, his horror-filled eyes set upon the towering dog before him. As soon as he stopped breathing, the dog fell back on four legs, turned and left the room without a single look at the amazed witnesses it left behind.

Thus passed the evil old man who had left nothing but misery in his wake.

# The Legend—or Legends—
# of the Wampus Cat

They are said to be present in many unsettled areas across the country—mysterious creatures that have long evaded human attention and defied traditional scientific classification. There are the famous Skunkape lurking in the swamps on the Florida–Alabama border and the Dog Lady howling at the full moon along with her pack in the woods of southern Michigan. There are the Frog People of Indiana; the Mothman of Ohio; and, of course, in practically every wild expanse from Louisiana to Washington State to Alaska, the legendary Big Foot. If you were to believe but half the tales circulating across the country, then the United States would be teeming with all manner of fabled beasts, a cryptozoologist's dream. Virginia would be no exception.

The Wampus Cat. In the wilds around the westernmost tip of the state, the massive, cat-like creature is said to roam the woods of the Appalachians, from eastern Tennessee and southern West Virginia, into Virginia's Wise and Lee counties, and to the national forests farther east. According to reports, it only ever appears at night, slinking at the edge of a town, shuffling through forests, raiding farms for cattle. No one can say when the first sighting occurred, but common stories place its origins among the ancient Cherokee. And while no one can guess at how many times it has been spotted since then, Wampus Cat sightings persist to this day, making it one of the region's most lasting folktales—but not one that many people can seem to agree upon.

First of all, there's the question of what exactly the Wampus Cat is. An enormous feline with burning eyes and a bizarre propensity for running about on its hind legs? A West Virginia witch whose dabbling in magic left her eternally trapped in a half-cat, half-human form? A mythological spirit from Cherokee folklore? There have been all sorts of explanations for the repeated sightings of this mysterious Appalachian creature.

What can be said about the Wampus Cat is that these sightings have been recurring for longer than anyone can remember. The presence of the creature in Cherokee legend suggests that it was lurking in the hills well before the early colonists arrived. Even then, there was some considerable variation in the creature's origins.

One version tells of a gigantic cat terrorizing a Cherokee village in the eastern part of Tennessee until the villagers elected their most courageous and skilled warrior to go out into the woods and hunt the creature down. The warrior went, ears to the ground, eyes locked on the shadows, spear at the ready. Whether he was in those hills for days, weeks or months, no one remembers, just as it is not known if he was the one who found the cat or the cat found him. Either way, hunter or quarry, he knew the moment he encountered the massive beast moving, partly concealed, amid the trees, the end of his quest was at hand.

Tightening his grip on his spear, the warrior took a mighty step and then lunged at the moving figure. But it lunged first. Darting out from among the trees, it was so fast that the warrior could not see it clearly. He spun and went flat as it dove overhead. He knew then it was big, impossibly big; if it was a cat, it was by far the largest cat he had ever

188 Ghost Stories of Virginia

seen. Undaunted, he rolled to his feet and turned to face the animal.

And then he lost his mind. It was not just the size of the cat—the impossibly unnatural size of it, standing between four and five feet at the shoulders, with a thick neck and massive legs, its wide jaws and spear-tip claws making the weapon in his shaking hands look like a toy. It was not just the physical appearance of the creature. It was something more—the roaring fire burning in its eyes, the hateful intelligence that shone from them, the overwhelming threat there. The warrior's last coherent thought was that the creature standing before him was not of this world. It was something greater, from some other place that he could not comprehend. The half-formed knowledge of this incomprehensible fact sent his mind reeling, and he turned and ran, screaming and babbling incoherently. When the villagers found him days later, he was still out of his mind. From his terrified stream of semi-conscious utterances, they gathered he had found the cat but that it was no normal beast of the woods. It quickly became obvious to them that the cat, just the sight of it, had reduced him to insanity.

Seeing how their best fighter had been reduced to a gibbering madman, none of the other men in the village was willing to go out and face the cat. The same could not be said of the women. It was the warrior's young wife who went out in search of the thing that had deprived her husband of his sanity. Knowledgeable in the ways of the Spirit World, this woman was sure that the thing in the woods was no mere cat. No animal of the earth could have affected her husband that way. She was convinced this was a demon spirit's work.

Before setting out, she went about protecting herself from the demon cat's potent magic. Her chants rang through the woods as she placed the cat mask over her face. The mask was made from the face of a real wildcat, as required by the spell she was casting. Thus protected, she headed out in search of the thing that had destroyed her husband's mind.

It was not difficult for her to find. The enchanted cat mask she wore connected her to her quarry, and she found her way to it without delay or hesitation. When she came upon the cat, it was lying in the middle of a grove, lazing in the shade, unaware of her approach. The woman crept up behind it, cat-like in her stealth, until she was standing an arm's length away from the beast. It was still not aware of her presence when she opened her mouth, raised her head to the sky and produced a huge roar that, for all its volume and ferocity, could have come from the mightiest lion. Terrified, the cat jumped to its feet and spun to face the woman in the cat mask. What it saw was not a woman in a cat mask, but an enormous feline, much larger than itself, towering over it on its two hind legs. Mortally afraid, the cat darted away and was never seen again. The woman, however, was changed forever. The magic of the mask took over, and in the moment she stared down the cat in the clearing she was transformed into the creature her quarry had seen—a looming feline beast standing on its two hind legs.

So it was that a big cat was replaced by an even bigger cat, and the legend of the Wampus Cat was born. The monstrous cat, instead of loping around on all fours, was often spotted walking on its two hind legs, moving with incredible speed through the wooded hills, through Cherokee villages and then later through the outskirts of Appalachian towns. Preserved by elemental Cherokee magic, the woman-turned-cat lived for centuries, and, according to some people, lives on to this day.

*The Wampus Cat appears only at night.*

The other version of the Cherokee legend involves the same subject—a woman dressing as a cat and heading into the woods—though her motivation is different. In this telling, the woman is not the wife of a mighty warrior but the wife of a philanderer who was not interested in much but the other women in their village. It was for this reason that his wife was suspicious whenever he went out on a hunt, and one day she decided to follow him. She put on the coat of a mountain lion and a mask with whiskers, a snout and pointed ears.

Disguised, she crept out after her husband and the band of hunters during one hunt, eager to see whether he broke off from them to join some woman in the woods. It may have indeed been the unfaithful man's plan, but she was found out before he had a chance to do it. The men were experienced hunters who knew the forest well, and the woman, encumbered by her costume and not used to moving with stealth, was not able to remain hidden for long. They found her out while taking a rest in a grove. She had just caught up with them and fell behind some bushes at the edge of the clearing, trying to hear what they were saying over her ragged breath. Perhaps she was fortunate that they did not mistake the shape in the woods for an actual mountain lion, or else she might have become the hunting expedition's first kill. Then again, given her ultimate fate, maybe she would have been better off if she had been mistaken for a wild beast.

She was dragged from the bushes and into the clearing. The hunters demanded to know why she was following them and in such a preposterous disguise. She spat back her response with a glare at her bewildered husband, telling them all she did not believe he was any kind of hunter and had followed them so she could catch him as he slunk off to be with whichever woman he was seeing. There was laughter, but the eldest hunter cut them off. He had spent many years of his life stalking prey in the woods and was known by all to have a deep bond with the wild. He understood the magic in the trees, the hills and the animals that dwelled there. There was also nothing in the world that was more sacred to him than the hunt, and he was outraged, now, that this woman would dare sully it with such ridiculous behavior.

Stepping forward, he spoke, and there was nothing kind or sympathetic in his voice. "You wear the skins of a mighty spirit," he said, fingering the costume draped around her shoulders. "But such a beast was not meant to stalk the comings and goings of an unfaithful husband." The woman's husband shrunk from the gaze of the great hunter. "Because you wish it, the spirits will grant you a far better disguise."

And then it happened, right before the eyes of the startled men. The woman was transformed into a great cat, standing as she had before, on two hind legs. One of the hunters was about to lunge at the creature but the elder held him back. "Let her be. From this day on, no hunter shall strike the cat that runs on two legs, for she is a woman of our village and will live long after all of us are gone." With these words, the Wampus Cat bounded away into the trees to spend coming centuries stalking the darker places.

When the early settlers came to the region, they had their own legend for the big cat that ran away on its hind legs when it was caught raiding their cattle. The Wampus Cat, they said, was actually an Appalachian witch who had fallen under the curse of her own magic. Before she had been forever transformed, she was a solitary woman living in the hills, a witch who was able to change herself into a cat. She routinely used this ability to take what she needed from the surrounding farmers. Morphing into a cat to sneak into farmers' homes, she crept into their bedrooms and cast a spell upon them so that nothing would wake them that night. From there, she made her way to the barn, where she took on her human form once again and made away with her pick of the livestock.

This strategy worked fine for her until the day a group of villagers got wise to her and laid a trap in a barn that she was in the process of robbing. Still in cat form, she had just entered the barn and was beginning to morph into her human form when the men hiding in the shadows sprung out at her. They grabbed her halfway through her transformation, breaking her concentration and disrupting her magic spell, so that she was still a cat, but an enormous cat standing on its hind legs. She let out a roar and broke free of her assailants, then bolted for the door with blinding speed.

Once in the woods, she tried to complete the spell and revert back to her human form only to discover she could not do so. She would be stuck in the body of the massive cat for the rest of her years. Raising her head to the sky, she let out a hellish howl that was heard over the trees and hills and through the Appalachian town. It was the first of many ear-splitting howls locals would hear with spine-tingling dread.

These are the legends of the Wampus Cat, all equally incredible and meant to explain the existence of a likewise incredible—and slightly absurd—folkloric creature: a mountain lion that, when frightened, runs away on its hind legs. In cryptozoological terms, only the Frog People of Indiana seem more incredible. Even so, those who claim to have seen the Wampus Cat or heard its tortured howling are less likely to laugh. According to their accounts, the beast still prowls the Appalachian back country. On the fringes of civilization, it ventures forth only at night, the cover of darkness obscuring its uncanny and altogether unnatural anatomy.

# The Black Sisters

The call had been no surprise. By that time, the carriage driver had come to expect the once-a-month summons to the Montgomery Female Academy, always late at night and always during a full moon. As before, he waited on the road in front of the school, quietly rubbing the crucifix that hung from his neck, cursing his hated profession and the financial necessity that compelled him to answer the call.

They appeared suddenly out of the darkness. The three women were dressed all in black, with long, formless skirts touching the ground, heavy black cloaks and thick midnight veils hanging from their queerly pitched hats. The driver felt an involuntary shudder course through his body and then gave his crucifix a final caress before hopping from the driver's seat. He went around his vehicle and opened the door, not saying a word as the three women climbed into the coach.

It was well past midnight, and the streets of Christiansburg were empty but for the lone carriage rolling forward. The driver knew his destination and went there with his dreaded cargo, wondering at all the rumors—suicides, insanity, the list of townsfolk struck with a sudden fear of the dark, the terrified students at the Montgomery Female Academy—all centered on the three women in his carriage. As he had countless times before, he wondered if there was any truth to the rumors; the driver was not the judgmental type, but he was still having trouble not assuming the worst of the so-called black sisters.

It was bad enough that they dressed the way they did, always draped entirely in darkness, their faces concealed behind veils. That alone would get chins wagging in

Christiansburg. But then there was everything else. They were almost never seen outside their house during the day. They supposedly came to life at night, striding through the streets with a troubling sense of purpose. "What are they doing up at all hours?" came the whispers. "It ain't natural for folk to be so busy after the sun's gone down."

Their nocturnal excursions fueled the public's suspicion of their queer dress and manner. It was not long before the three women became pariahs, accused of all sorts of fiendish behavior. Someone heard from someone else that there were girls at the academy waking up in their dormitory beds in the middle of the night to find three black figures standing before their beds. Or a friend of a friend was up later than usual and stumbled upon the trio creeping around some Christiansburg resident's house, spying through the windows.

Then there was what happened to John Snead, the newcomer to town who had gotten a job as a teacher at the academy soon after the sisters' arrival. Alone in his room, he had doused himself in kerosene and lit a match. The screams brought the other teachers running from their quarters. When they burst into his bedroom, he was engulfed in flames, convulsing upon the floor. The teachers managed to put out the fire, but it was too late for Snead. He died three hours later.

It may have still been possible for the driver, normally a pragmatic and rational man, to dismiss such accounts as bad luck and the gossip of superstitious minds—if, that is, it was not for the monthly rides. Who were these women, clad in black, who insisted on being driven to the same cemetery when the moon was full? What were they doing out there among those tombstones while he waited by his carriage?

These moonlit forays, if nothing else, convinced the driver there was something very wrong with the sisters.

These once-a-month trips gave the driver more contact with the black sisters than most of the other townsfolk in Christiansburg. The truth was that although there were many stories floating around about them, most of the stories were based on the frightened hearsay of another. What was known was that one of the sisters, Virginia Wardlaw, had been appointed the headmistress of the Montgomery Female Academy because the sisters' great-aunt, 93-year-old Oceana Seaborn Pollock, owned the school. What was also known was that, before arriving at Christiansburg, all three sisters had been teachers and administrators at another girls' school in Murfreesboro, Tennessee. Although no one had any reliable information on their tenure in Tennessee, the rumor was that they had planted some evil in Murfreesboro and were working to the same end in Virginia.

Arriving at the cemetery, the driver drew his carriage to a halt. "We're here."

But the sisters did not need to be told. The carriage door was already open, and they were getting out. Draped in black, they all looked like the same person to him. Two walked to the cemetery gate while the other approached him. A thick voice slithered out from under the veil. "Wait for us here. We'll return soon."

The man nodded and watched the three figures disappear into the darkness of the cemetery. He sat and waited, occasionally casting a nervous glance at the moonlit graveyard. He knew from experience that they would not be back for about half an hour, doing God-only-knew-what. Fidgeting in his carriage, he tried turning his thoughts to other things, but his

*Who were these women, clad in black, who insisted on being driven to the same cemetery when the moon was full?*

curiosity was getting the better of him as it had in previous trips. He had told friends and family about the trips to the cemetery, and it became just another reason to suspect the black sisters. Countless times he had been asked the question that he also asked himself: *What are they doing out there?*

He decided that night that it was time to find out. Whatever they did in the cemetery, he knew they would be doing it for some time yet. The idea of being caught spying terrified him. Who knew what these women were capable of?

But he told himself that the moon was high, and once inside he would be able to see them from a distance. He would take cover going from headstone to headstone until he was close enough to make out what was going on. *No problem*, he told himself, running low up to the cemetery gate.

He heard them before he saw them—three voices drifting in from a distance, chanting with a strange cadence, a lilting, almost melodic rhythm in a language he did not understand. Or did not understand literally, anyway. On some other level, he comprehended the way the undulating voices were like worms under his skin, the way his legs trembled with every step he took. He could not understand the language, but he could hear the malice in the intonations, and his gut was telling him to turn around.

But he kept moving forward, darting from tombstone to tombstone, until the black sisters came into sight. He could see them in the silver light. They were standing side by side before a grave with their backs to him. For the most part, they were motionless as they chanted, but every now and then one of them would raise her arms to the sky, another reaching into the folds of a black cloak to sprinkle something over the gravesite.

The driver did not watch for long. Unable to bear the spectacle before him, he turned and crept back to his carriage, where he waited in silence for the black sisters to conclude their business. Whatever that was. The next day, while sitting around the breakfast table with his family, he would have problems describing what had seen. Were they singing? Not exactly. Were they praying? Perhaps there was a ritual feel to what he had seen; it could have been religious. What language where they speaking? He had no idea. The only thing the driver could say for sure was that whatever they were up to, it was not good. He remembered the dread he felt as he watched the black sisters, and swore the Devil was in the cemetery that night.

It went down as another page in the sisters' dark and growing list of peculiarities. Vowing that he wanted no part of whatever wicked rituals they were playing out at the cemetery, the carriage driver swore that was the last time he would pick them up for their monthly ride. As it turned out, he was never called upon for the task again, for the black sisters moved out of town before the next full moon.

There was a palpable sense of relief at their departure, which was generally considered long overdue. A number of Christiansburg residents had been vocal in their opposition to the sisters, and it was not only because of the fear and suspicion they spread through town, but it was about the school.

Ever since Virginia Wardlaw had taken over as headmistress, more and more girls had dropped out of the academy. An ever-growing number of parents were leveling charges against the sisters, claiming the college dormitories had traumatized their daughters. They voiced complaint after tearful complaint of harassment at the hands of the black-clad women. The sisters, it was said, regularly crept into the girls' rooms after lights out. They would gather at a specific student's bedside, where they would stand, sometimes for the better part of an hour, muttering in low, unintelligible voices.

As the number of students dropping out increased, the school's financial situation worsened. Unpaid bills accumulated along with the mounting controversy and dark supposition. Then one day the sisters just vanished. Without a warning or a trace, they were gone. Christiansburg would never see the black sisters again. But it would hear of them.

In late November 1909, a few years after they had disappeared from Christiansburg, the sisters emerged in New York newspapers at the center of a suspected homicide in a New Jersey home. The victim's name was Ocey Snead, cousin of John Snead—the teacher who had killed himself in Christiansburg—and, as the authorities discovered, daughter of Caroline Martin, the eldest of the black sisters. At the time, she had been sharing the house with her aunt, Virginia Wardlaw.

Ocey's body had been found in the bathroom, partly submerged in a half-filled tub. She was crouched in a fetal position, her head under the water, her body gruesomely emaciated, weighing, it was believed, no more than 80 pounds at the time of death. There was a suicide note pinned to her bathrobe. It read: "Last year my little daughter died; other near and dear ones have gone before. I have been prostrated with illness for a long time. When you read this I will have committed suicide. Do not grieve over me. Rejoice with me that death brings a blessed relief from pain and suffering greater than I can bear."

And yet investigators had reason to doubt the veracity of the letter. A closer look at the evidence suggested there was more to the case.

The first experts at the scene determined that the young woman had been dead for over a day, at least, while the call by Virginia Wardlaw had just been made that afternoon. When confronted with this information, Wardlaw claimed she had not seen her niece since the day before, a dubious assertion considering this testimony meant she had not used the one and only bathroom in the house for a 24-hour period. One question led to another, and Wardlaw was quickly taken into custody. It was the subsequent investigation that brought the black sisters' morbid history to light.

When questioned, Wardlaw's neighbors revealed that the night before Ocey Snead's body had been discovered, two other women, both dressed in black, had been seen entering the house. Detectives learned that Ocey had been married and was living in a house in Brooklyn until quite recently. Then Wardlaw and her two sisters moved in with the young couple, and the husband ran off soon after. Not long after her husband had fled, Ocey took out a generous life insurance policy in which the black sisters were listed as the main beneficiaries.

The police spoke with the lawyers who had drafted Ocey's life insurance policy and drawn up her new will; by their statements, it was obvious that something was wrong when they visited the house. There, they found a visibly weakened and emotionally distraught Ocey Snead, who seemed terrified of the three women in black she lived with. It was a surreal experience for these legal advocates, who also went on the record as saying that as Ocey Snead was putting her signature on the legal documents, the black sisters were sitting around her, muttering strange incantations and making bizarre gesticulations. There was a minute or two during the meeting when the lawyers found themselves alone with Ocey, at which point the young woman hissed her desperate plea, telling them that she was being starved and deprived of her medication, begging the men to get her out. For reasons we can only guess at, they did nothing to aid the frantic woman.

*Ocey Snead in bed with her infant daughter*

The new information implicated Wardlaw's two sisters in the crime, and it was not long after this news that the tale of their travels through Tennessee and Virginia was unearthed. Before they had arrived at the Montgomery Female Academy in Christiansburg, they had worked at the Soule Female College in Murfreesboro, Tennessee. Although there were parallels in the way their stories unraveled in the two towns, it took much longer for them to become pariahs in Tennessee. As it turned out, their pariah status had a lot to do with Caroline Martin, Ocey's mother.

Wardlaw was offered a position as headmistress of the Soule Female College in 1892, a job that she took on with diligence and skill. Quickly winning the respect of her peers at Soule, she hired her sister, the recently widowed Mary Snead, in 1897. The two sisters were not without their detractors. Some people commented on their reclusive tendencies and the way they always wore black. But they apparently did their work well, staying out of other people's business, and were by and large accepted in Murfreesboro.

That was until 1901, when Caroline Martin arrived in town. She was the eldest sister and, like the other two, was clad entirely in black. Her arrival marked the advent of sinister times at the college. Soule fell apart in much the same way as the Montgomery Female Academy in Virginia would. Weird stories began spreading about the sisters, who now seemed to be completely under the control of the eldest sister. Whenever they were seen, it was together, either drifting through town in the middle of the night, or else walking in utter silence through the rooms and halls of Soule College—always in black, always with some grim and mysterious purpose.

In Murfreesboro, Caroline Martin had a personal maid who was the source of no small amount of gossip. Closer to the black-clad matriarch than anyone else in town, this maid was eager to spread word of her strange and disturbed employer. She described an isolated woman of extraordinary slovenliness and bizarre habits who never let anyone in to clean up her sty of a room, and who slept with a loaded double barreled shotgun next to her pillow. The maid told stories about how Caroline Martin stayed in for days on end, wearing the same reeking, threadbare nightgown, never bathing or combing her knotted mass of hair. At night, chants in some

204 Ghost Stories of Virginia

unknown language could be heard coming from her room, punctuated by maniacal cackling.

Soule Female College began to collapse. Suddenly and inexplicably short on money, the school began falling behind on bill payments. All the while, students were vacating in droves, frightened off by the unsettling habits of the black sisters, who now never ventured out during daylight hours and grew detached from their work in the school. Increasingly, students reported waking up to see the three sisters standing over their bed in the darkness, murmuring a strange litany in a foreign language. Then, without warning, the black sisters were gone. The year was 1905, 13 years after Wardlaw first arrived.

They did not last nearly as long at their next stop, as schoolteachers and administrators in Christiansburg, but their behavior was much the same. While looking into the immolation of young John Snead in Virginia, investigators discovered that he, like his cousin, had taken out a life insurance policy shortly before he died, in which the black sisters were listed as the principal beneficiaries.

Mary Snead ended up pleading guilty to manslaughter. Placed in the custody of her son, Albert, on his secluded Colorado ranch, she spent the rest of her days in the shadow of the Rocky Mountains, ruminating on her role in the murders of Ocey and John Snead. Caroline Martin, the suspected mastermind behind the black sisters' crimes, was locked up in the New Jersey state prison. There, she was quickly deemed unstable and transferred to the State Hospital for the Insane. She died soon after that.

As for Virginia Wardlaw, the most socialized of the black sisters—who had been an able schoolteacher and headmistress before she was reunited with Caroline Martin in Tennessee—she simply stopped eating. Awaiting trial in prison for her role in the murders, she starved herself to death before the gavel fell on the first day of the proceedings. Her body was buried in the Sunset Cemetery in Christiansburg, a short distance from the school she had once presided over.

The black sisters were permanently cast apart—one exiled, one confined, one starved. Their story faded into relative obscurity soon after it stopped getting headlines in the New York papers, regarded as that of just another three morally corrupt individuals who were willing to do anything for money. In the eyes of cynical readers, there was no shortage of people like the black sisters.

But not everyone was about to dismiss them so quickly; there were those who looked past their murderous motives, to the strange behavior that had made them so feared in Tennessee and Virginia. The uniformity of their dress, their nocturnal habits, the harassment of female students, their fascination with cemeteries, the bizarre chanting. How did they manage to convince John and Ocey Snead to take out life insurance policies and list them as the beneficiaries?

The black sisters have since taken their place in Virginia lore. Sometimes they are described as nothing more than three greedy women devoid of scruples, willing even to murder family for money. Other accounts make them into something more. References to Satanism and witchcraft suggest such women employed the most evil forces, the blackest of black magic, to accomplish their nefarious ends.

There are claims, it must also be noted, that the evil of the black sisters persists, that on certain nights, when the moon is full, three women shrouded in dark garments drift through the quiet streets of Christiansburg. Their feet make no sound, but their voices are audible, three female voices coming together in a foreign chant that freezes the air around them. They have also been spotted indoors. The main building of the Montgomery Female College was torn down some time ago, and the Christiansburg Middle School was built on the site. Nevertheless, according to some people, there is reason to believe that the black sisters have transferred to the new school. Or some part of the black sisters, anyway, for over the years many odd sightings have been reported. Translucent apparitions, arriving in a silver mist drifting down the halls, vanishing faces peering from windows, black shapes darting into empty classrooms—the black sisters are apparently still very active in the Christiansburg school.

Students and parents need not worry. No one has expressed any interest in hiring the sisters on again.

# The End

# Collect The Entire Series!

More Ghost Stories books will be available in the months ahead.
Check with your local bookseller or order direct.
U.S. readers call 1-800-518-3541. In Canada, call 1-800-661-9017.
www.lonepinepublishing.com